Robert Motherwell, Abstraction, and Philosophy

I0474432

Employing an interdisciplinary approach, this book breaks new ground by considering how Robert Motherwell's abstract expressionist art is indebted to Alfred North Whitehead's highly original process metaphysics.

Motherwell first encountered Whitehead and his work as a philosophy graduate student at Harvard University, and he continued to espouse Whitehead's processist theories as germane to his art throughout his life. This book examines how Whitehead's process philosophy—inspired by quantum theory and focusing on the ongoing ingenuity of dynamic forces of energy rather than traditional views of inert substances—set the stage for Motherwell's future art.

This book will be of interest to scholars in twentieth-century modern art, philosophy of art and aesthetics, and art history.

Robert Hobbs has served as associate professor at Cornell University, USA, and long-term visiting professor at Yale University, USA; he has also held the Thalhimer Endowed Chair of American Art at Virginia Commonwealth University, USA.

Routledge Focus on Art History and Visual Studies

Robert Motherwell, Abstraction, and Philosophy

Robert Hobbs

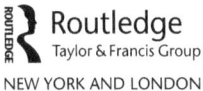

NEW YORK AND LONDON

First published 2020
by Routledge
52 Vanderbilt Avenue, New York, NY 10017

and by Routledge
2 Park Square, Milton Park, Abingdon, Oxon, OX14 4RN

Routledge is an imprint of the Taylor & Francis Group, an informa business

Library of Congress Cataloging-in-Publication Data
A catalog record for this title has been requested

ISBN: 978-0-367-21044-1 (hbk)
ISBN: 978-0-367-51142-5 (pbk)
ISBN: 978-0-429-26508-2 (ebk)

Typeset in Times New Roman
by Deanta Global Publishing Services, Chennai, India

This book is gratefully dedicated to
Renate Ponsold Motherwell

Contents

Acknowledgments

As a graduate student researching Robert Motherwell's personal archives in Greenwich, CT, I first met this artist on October 24, 1974, the day he returned home after five heart operations. At the time I was investigating his magisterial series of *Elegies to the Spanish Republic* for my dissertation. Because of his grave situation, Motherwell focused on the one person he believed to have been crucial for his development as an abstract artist. "My work is profoundly indebted to Alfred North Whitehead," he said, before conceding, "Perhaps he is too difficult for anyone to figure out the connections." My initial response was to pursue this extraordinarily generous insight, but my already approved dissertation topic, with Donald Kuspit as its able director, took me in a different direction. Over the years, as I have researched a range of modern and postmodern topics, I have continued to reflect on Motherwell's remarkably candid disclosure. Several years ago, I decided to pursue his revelation by examining his graduate student days in Harvard's philosophy department, including his early contacts with Whitehead, to ascertain the overall impact this process philosopher's work had on Motherwell's art.

Because I am neither a specialist in process theory nor a philosopher, I contacted the respected Center for Process Studies at Claremont School of Theology requesting the recommendation of a philosopher well versed in Whitehead's views on art, who would be willing to critique my completed manuscript. The Center contacted on my behalf Dr. George Allan, Professor Emeritus of Philosophy at Dickinson College and author of *Modes of Learning: Whitehead's Metaphysics and the Stages of Education* (State University of New York Press, 2013). Professor Allan graciously agreed to read my essay, and he provided several worthwhile suggestions while approving my use of Whitehead's ideas.

Since the 1970s I have been fortunate in being able to expand on my initial research on Motherwell's art in exhibitions and essays, beginning with co-curating in 1975 *Subjects of the Artists: New York Painting 1941–1947* for the Downtown Branch of the Whitney Museum of American Art in 1975 and coauthoring in 1977 with Barbara Cavaliere the essay "Against a Newer Laocoon" for *Arts Magazine*. This essay, which has subsequently been used as a text in undergraduate and graduate courses, underscores substantial differences between critic Clement Greenberg's formalist approach to abstract expressionism and the artists' statements about meaningful content inhering in their abstract forms. In 1976 I wrote essays on Motherwell's *Elegies* and *Open* series for his first European retrospective, which was curated by Jürgen Harten for the Städtische Kunsthalle, Düsseldorf; and in 1978 I co-curated with Gail Levin *Abstract Expressionism: The Formative Years*, which opened at Cornell University's Herbert F. Johnson Museum of Art before being shown at the Whitney. Our coauthored catalogue was later republished by Cornell University Press. My essay "Early Abstract Expressionism and Surrealism" was published by the US College Art Association's *Art Journal* in 1985; "The Victorian Unconscious: Tonalist Sources for Abstract Expressionism" was included in Paul Schimmel's 1986 exhibition catalogue *The Interpretive Link: Abstract Surrealism into Abstract Expressionism*; "Motherwell's *Opens*: Heidegger, Mallarmé, and Zen" became part of the 2009 multiauthored *Robert Motherwell: Open*, which was published by London 21 Publishing Ltd., and my essay "Krasner, Mitchell, and Frankenthaler: Nature as Metonym" was included in Joan Marter, ed., *Women of Abstract Expressionism*, published by the Denver Art Museum in association with Yale University Press in 2016. In addition, I have presented papers pertaining to Motherwell's art and thought at annual US College Art Association meetings and have participated in a number of museum symposia on abstract expression. These publications, papers, and talks have served as excellent opportunities to share my ideas while obtaining worthwhile feedback from other scholars; thus, they form a meaningful background for my present study.

    In addition to my involvement with Motherwell's art, I have undertaken sustained investigations of two other abstract expressionists and their art. My work on Lee Krasner resulted in two different monographs (1993 and 1999) and one retrospective (1999). My exploration of Richard Pousette-Dart's art was undertaken in conjunction with the very pleasant task of co-curating with Joanne Kuebler the artist's first retrospective (1990) and contributing to its complementary monograph, in addition to curating a gallery exhibition for Knoedler and Company in New York City (2008) and writing the accompanying catalogue. As one of my esteemed professors Joseph Sloane was fond of saying, "A person who knows only one artist's work does not really know that artist at all," as his way of emphasizing the crucial need for comparisons between members of the same and different generations are crucial if one is to make informed historical judgments. And so, I would like to think that my work on both Krasner and Pousette-Dart has contributed, albeit indirectly, to my understanding of Motherwell's many contributions.

In my analyses of abstract expressionist art, I have gratefully depended on the expertise of a number of art historians, curators, and critics and have benefited enormously from many enjoyable and fruitful exchanges with them. These individuals include the aforementioned individuals as well as the following: Craig Adcock, Lawrence Alloway, David Anfam, Dore Ashton, E.A. Carmean, Mary Ann Caws, Claude Cernuschi, Heidi Colsman-Freyberger, David Craven, Isabelle Dervaux, Elsa Fine, Jack Flam, Stephen Foster, Ann Gibson, Ellen Landau, Elizabeth Langhorne, Gerrit Lansing, Joan Marter, S.A. Mansbach, Kent Minturn, Stephen Polcari, Barbara Rose, Irving Sandler, Martica Sawin, Katy Siegel, Patterson Sims, and Howard Singerman, among others; artists Peter Sacks and John Scofield, who for several years was Motherwell's studio assistant; philosopher Barbara Meyerson; museum directors Thomas N. Armstrong III, Thomas W. Leavitt, and Alan Shestack; and gallerists Robert Delaney, Ann Freedman, and Bernard Jacobson.

Working with Jack Flam, Katy Rogers, and Tim Clifford's handsome and useful three-volume tome *Robert Motherwell Paintings and Collages: A Catalogue Raisonné, 1941–1991* has been most gratifying. And I greatly appreciate that Flam in his capacity as President and CEO of the Dedalus Foundation was able to provide permission to cite Motherwell's statements in the present book, thereby ensuring this artist's inimical voice a central role. Monica McTighe, Dedalus's Archivist, has been most responsive to my many questions, and I thank her for her help.

At Routledge/Taylor & Francis, it has indeed been a great privilege and pleasure to work first with Isabella Vitti, Editor of Art History & Visual Studies, and then with Katie Armstrong, Editorial Assistant, Art History & Visual Studies. In addition, Joanna Hardern, Production Editor, Routledge and Jayanthi Chander, Project Manager, Deanta Global have been most assiduous in editing this manuscript, and I am most appreciative of their pertinacity. All have been highly professional, and all have remained keenly aware of the importance of this undertaking and have helped to find ways to ensure it becomes a reality. Three anonymous readers contacted by Vitti read the manuscript and made several excellent suggestions.

Over the years the research position of Rhoda Thalhimer Endowed Chair of American Art has permitted the necessary time to undertake this and other projects. It has also ensured the support of able graduate students awarded Thalhimer Research Assistantships whose contributions have proven invaluable. For this project I have been able to rely on the conscientious help of Timothy Andrus, Nicole De Armendi, Ashley Duhrkoop, Owen Duffy, and John Hebble.

I recall with great fondness the warm hospitality Robert Motherwell and Renate Ponsold extended to me during the 1975–1976 academic year, when I was living in their guesthouse while serving as a full-time lecturer at Yale University. During that year, Anne Coffin Hanson, Chair of Yale's Art History Department, supported the idea of an upper-level undergraduate seminar on abstract expressionism, and the thoughtful conversations with the students in this class, particularly Debbie Gee and Mollie McNickle, is a memory I continue to cherish. Finally, my profound thanks to Jean Crutchfield for her unwavering belief in this project.

1 Introduction

This book proposes a new way of thinking about the art of abstract expressionist Robert Motherwell (1915–1991) based on his assimilation of the groundbreaking theories of Alfred North Whitehead (1861–1947) during 1937–1938, when he was enrolled as a graduate student in Harvard University's philosophy department. It is also concerned with his later personalization of these ideas as a foundation for his art. In the twentieth century, when analytical and anti-speculative theories dominated the field of philosophy, Whitehead's metaphysics, which he began formulating in the mid-1920s,[1] epitomized a distinctly different alternative. Representing the first such inquiry into this seminal connection between philosopher and painter and by extension abstract expressionism, my investigation looks at how Whitehead's contributions to process philosophy,[2] inspired by quantum physics and focused on an ongoing creativity of dynamic forces of energy rather than traditional views of inert materials, set the stage for Motherwell's future art

This study also examines how Motherwell's understanding of Whitehead's ideas became a major factor in his reinterpretation of the surrealist technique of psychic automatism. Motherwell renamed this process plastic automatism and viewed it throughout his life as a seminal "principle" and not a style.[3] For Motherwell, this improvisatory method was a mutually collaborative and catalytic activity taking place between artists and their media rather than remaining an artist-centered technique, as the surrealist interpreted it.[4] In the early 1940s Motherwell worked with his close friend and fellow burgeoning abstract expressionist William Baziotes under the guidance of the Chilean architect-turned-surrealist painter, Roberto Matta Echaurren, to proselytize the merits of plastic automatism to several artists who became key abstract expressionists. Because of their efforts and because their use of automatism as a medium-based process enabled them to achieve distinctly different individual styles, Motherwell's Whiteheadian views toward this creative approach need to be regarded as integral to abstract expressionist theory.[5]

My self-assigned task has been to rethink Motherwell's work in relationship to Whitehead's thought, one that has become less burdensome than I originally anticipated. One reason for this new approachability is the pertinence of Whitehead's ideas for a number of well-known theorists and scholars, many of them notable postmodernists, such as Gilles Deleuze, Donna Haraway, Bruno Latour, and Isabelle Stengers. Another reason for the enhanced relevancy of Whitehead's philosophy is the establishment of the Center for Process Studies at the Claremont School of Theology in 1973, with the express mission of focusing on the work of Whitehead and his former research assistant Charles Hartshorne. Since the early 1990s, this Center has published a most useful biannual, peer-reviewed journal devoted to the contributions of Whitehead and Hartshorne. In addition to these publications, there has been a steady stream of in-depth and useful philosophic analyses and assessments of Whitehead's thought.

Even though Motherwell is the abstract expressionist with the greatest formal training in philosophy, the extensive and often insightful published material on him provides only passing summaries of his time as a graduate student in philosophy at Harvard. However, as I intend to show, this fecund period enabled him to appreciate artistic creativity in Whiteheadian terms as life's ultimate principle. Although Whitehead had retired from teaching in the spring of 1937 before Motherwell enrolled the next fall in Harvard's graduate program, he remained a viable presence in Cambridge, due in part to his regular Sunday night salons at his home in Cambridge. At such times Whitehead would expound on his theories with wit and charm.[6] In addition to these evenings, Whitehead delivered during 1937–1938 six public lectures at Wellesley intended in his words "to condense…those features of my Harvard lectures…incompletely presented in my published works,"[7] and Motherwell attended a number of these talks.[8] Together with the addition of two papers given at the University of Chicago in 1933 and a statement about philosophy's goals, these lectures were published in 1938 under the title *Modes of Thought*, which Motherwell purchased and read.

In addition to his casual and more formal contacts with Whitehead, Motherwell was able to build on his undergraduate major in philosophy at Stanford University and his paper (now lost) on another process philosopher, the French late-nineteenth and twentieth-century thinker Henri Bergson. In *Creative Evolution* (1907), Bergson originated the concept of *élan vital*, the vital impulse responsible for the sustained advancement of all living forms, with humans clearly situated at their summit as the planet's reason for being. In the early twentieth century—a time of enormous and almost constant change—Bergson was revered for considering intuition as a way to embrace life's essence and for defining the related term duration as "a multiplicity of moments bound to each other by a unity which goes through them like a thread."[9] Although Motherwell acquired a number of Bergson's books over the years, he only mentioned this theorist once in his many writings and interviews. For this reason, the best way to think about Bergson and Motherwell is to consider this theorist and his approach as background for Whitehead's more complex metaphysics, which are predicated on a view of the universe's far-reaching creativity and a concern for humanity as an integral part of the world but not its pinnacle.

In the 1930s Motherwell acquired a total of four books by Whitehead and he kept them throughout his life even though he went through four marriages and the consequent breakups of his household entailed by three divorces. Later, he obtained three more of Whitehead's works. Among the volumes in Motherwell's library was Whitehead's great metaphysical trilogy—*Science and the Modern World*, *Process and Reality*, and *Adventures of Ideas*—thus providing him with ample opportunities to familiarize himself with their main points. Although Whitehead was not an aesthetician, on several occasions he wrote about poetry and more rarely on the visual arts.[10] Most importantly, Whitehead considered poetry to "express deep intuitions of mankind penetrating into what is universal in concrete fact,"[11] thus enabling some scholars to point to the aesthetic character of his metaphysics. Whitehead went on to explain the importance of aesthetics for his philosophy, "The metaphysical doctrine…finds the foundations of the world in aesthetic experience, rather than—as with Kant—in the cognitive and conceptive experience," adding, "All order is therefore aesthetic order."[12]

A devoted reader of poetry, Motherwell found Whitehead's comments about poetry and aesthetics persuasive and useful. In his paper "On Not Becoming an Academic," presented in 1986 as part of Harvard University's 350th anniversary celebration, Motherwell recalled his early acquaintance with both Whitehead the individual and his formidable philosophy:

> Though Alfred North Whitehead had retired the academic year before, his presence and ideas permeated the philosophy department at Harvard, and through tracking down, in his scattered writings, a paragraph here or there, I came to understand the philosophical nature of abstraction, which was a crucial idea for an aspiring young modernist painter in the 1930s to apprehend, saving me those years of doubt and confusion that most painters of the period had to go through in slowly breaking away from the representational modes in which they had been trained.[13]

Motherwell followed this narrative account by emphasizing even more how Whitehead and his time at Harvard had enabled him so quickly to accept and practice abstract art:

The clarity of those insights on Whitehead's part allowed me within six months of when I began painting full-time (for the rest of my life) in 1941 to paint a now celebrated small work called *The Little Spanish Prison* (Collection, Museum of Modern Art, New York). Who could have guessed that in the Graduate School of Philosophy at Harvard, I should come across perceptions by a professional philosopher and mathematician that would play a crucial, though far from the only role, in my development as a painter?[14]

Although he refers in this statement to the ideas that enabled him to embrace abstract art, Motherwell does not mention the time when he first became entranced with modern art's distinctly abstract components. By all accounts this occurred in the fall of 1935, when he was an undergraduate student at Stanford University and was invited to the home of the art collectors Michael and Sarah Stein in Palo Alto. This opportunity enabled him to see at first hand major fauvist and cubist works. That same year he was able to hear Gertrude Stein lecture at Stanford University on literature and painting. Over time these events had a huge impact on his willingness to become an abstract painter. As he acknowledged on a number of occasions, the extraordinary Matisse paintings in the Stein collection, including the important Fauvist *Woman with a Hat* (*Femme au chapeau*), won him over immediately and completely. That same fall he was enrolled in a year-long course in French symbolist poetry that included Stéphane Mallarmé and other late nineteenth-century French symbolist poets, including Charles Baudelaire (a particular favorite), Arthur Rimbaud, Paul Valéry, and Paul Verlaine. During this time, he also read works by such American poets as Hart Crane, e.e. cummings, Ezra Pound, Marianne Moore, and Wallace Stevens.[15] Thus, Motherwell had opportunities to appreciate the visual and verbal range of abstraction in modern art and poetry.

In addition to Whitehead, Motherwell embraced in the late 1940s and 1950s the work of this theorist's first Harvard PhD student, the mid-twentieth-century philosopher Susanne K. Langer (1895–1985), whose mid-century writings were often used as texts in college courses in aesthetics and were even highly recommended by such an eminent art historian as Columbia University professor Meyer Schapiro.[16] My investigation of Langer's later elaborations of Whitehead's thought, with which Motherwell familiarized himself during the 1940s when he was a practicing artist in New York City, underscore their significance for substantiating his belief that individual artworks are integral symbols comprised of mutually supportive elements.

In the fall of 1942 and the winter of 1943, with the emotional support of Matta and the help of Baziotes, Motherwell was able to communicate to a group of New York artists his own version of psychic automatism.[17] In doing so he was supported by Matta's knowledge of Sigmund Freud's theories and view of the mind as a three-dimensional inscape, a realm unique to each individual. This concept was generated by the Victorian poet Gerard Manley Hopkins, even though Matta later diverted from this view of the preconscious mind as territory to be conquered and characterized it in terms of thoughts below the level of consciousness and energy. Motherwell presented the aesthetic theory of psychic automatism as a process to such artists as the renowned teacher of modern art practices, the German expatriate Hans Hofmann (then in his sixties), as well as more experienced and slightly older contemporaries in New York, including Peter Busa, Gerome Kamrowski, and Jackson Pollock. Motherwell did so in order to promote the advantages of his own interpretation of this surrealist technique and thereby stage, together with Matta and Baziotes, a "palace coup" intended to show up the older generation of established expatriate European surrealists, then living in New York, as being out of touch with their artistic movement's foundational concept, which their chief apologist André Breton had characterized in terms of the mind's way of operating.[18]

Since Hofmann and Pollock became leading first-generation abstract expressionists, and since Motherwell communicated these ideas in social settings first to Lee Krasner, Pollock's partner, and later Mark Rothko, he subsequently came to believe that the concept of plastic automatism, together with his and his friends' efforts to introduce it to these and other artists in New York, was a key factor in abstract expressionism's development.[19] Most likely these older and more experienced artists were willing to accept Motherwell's explanations because his formal education in philosophy enabled him to express his ideas with impressive authority. Plastic automatism provided one means for differentiating the new Americans' more democratic collaborations between artists and their materials from the methods espoused by many well-established European surrealists and constructivists, who believed themselves and their subconscious minds to be acting unilaterally when they were creating and consequently were relegating their media to auxiliary status. Motherwell's two major texts on plastic automatism, based, as I intend to demonstrate, largely on Whitehead's theories, include the paper later published under the title "The Modern Painter's World," which he presented at the 1944 conference entitled "Arts Plastique," part of Mount Holyoke's "Pontigny en Amérique" summer program, and the essay "The Significance of Miró," published in the May 1959 issue of *Art News*, then a cutting-edge periodical.

Whitehead's process philosophy is a new cosmological perspective concerning ongoing conjunctions of forces, and he is one of the first twentieth-century theorists to attempt a conscious and meaningful reconciliation between quantum theory and the humanities.[20] In 1925 Whitehead explains his basic approach to process theory, based on self-selecting forces grouping together to achieve novel units. The *actual entity* (a Whiteheadian key term) making up this highly conceptual yet improvisational type of art is predicated on the congregating forces that are the art object per se in the following way. "[O]ne of the most hopeful lines of explanation [of quantum theory], Whitehead writes, is to assume that an electron does not continuously traverse its path in space. The alternative notion as to its mode of existence is that it appears as a series of discrete positions in space which it occupies for successive durations of time. It is as though an automobile, moving at the average rate of thirty miles an hour along a road, did not traverse the road continuously; but appeared successively at the successive milestones, remaining for two minutes at each milestone."[21]

According to philosopher and science historian Michael Epperson:

> Whitehead's references to the quantum theory as an exemplification of his cosmological scheme…pertain to three related concepts—the first one best associated with the "old" quantum theory of Planck and Einstein as applied to Bohr's 1913 atomic model, and the other two best associated with the "new" quantum theory of Heisenberg, Schrödinger, Bohr, et al., typically referred to as the Copenhagen Interpretation.[22]

Quantum theory, with its seemingly unpredictable jumps or shifts, enabled Whitehead to speculate about a spontaneously self-generated dynamism, i.e., energy, as the ultimate state of the universe.[23] In addition to his own work and personal impact on abstract expressionist theory, Motherwell's foundation in Whiteheadian theory enables us to view his art in particular and abstract expressionism in general as participating in one of the twentieth century's most revolutionary views of the universe, quantum physics, which relinquishes the older conception of the world in terms of static components to the new standpoint of considering the universe as comprising dynamic forces.[24] Whitehead often referred to this earlier attitude, with its origins in Aristotle's theories, as scientific materialism, an elemental systematic type of materialism.

When Motherwell's art and abstract expressionism are understood in terms of Whitehead's process philosophy, this type of work ceases to be a late version of romanticism, involving the deification of artists and their emotional expressions as the subject of their work, which has been one of the mainstays of many abstract expressionist studies. In Whitehead's process philosophy, this traditional romantic-era hierarchy is leveled, and artists become one set of factors among others, so that they work in tandem with their media to forge spontaneously achieved conjunctions that seem—almost like the subatomic particles that inspired Whitehead—to have a will of their own. Consequently, creativity in a Whiteheadian universe is egalitarian and dependent on fortuitous connections on a par with the connected forces this philosopher calls *actual entities*—no doubt characterized as *actual* because of the belief that dynamic velocities of elements rather than static materials form the universe's essential core. Whitehead then refers to these spontaneously self-created congregations of energies as *feelings*—a term applicable to both organic and nonorganic life, making it difficult at first to comprehend. Motherwell often used the word feeling to account for the impulsively formed aggregations of elements that, according to Whitehead's theories, function very much like subatomic particles.

This felt quality—the spontaneous attraction of disparate elements—is of paramount importance to Motherwell and his critical views of his own work in particular and abstract expressionism in general since it enabled him to comprehend his art and the work of his stylistic associates as being not so much imbued with their own particular emotions as it is involved in a two-step openness to feeling that comprises (1) the spontaneous mutual attraction of artist, medium, and consequent individual elements forming the artwork, and (2) viewers' responses to the ensuing relationships comprising a given work. In support of this concept that individual works of art are capable of communicating their own feelings, Motherwell wrote, 'Painting that does not radiate feeling is not worth looking at. The deepest—and rarest—of grown-up pleasures is true feeling.'²⁵ While art writers focusing on Motherwell's work have perceived a tension between feeling and thought as well as instinct and intellect, I contend that Whitehead's theories about spontaneous self-generating congregations based on feelings provided a way for Motherwell to resolve the two. In addition, it opened the way for thoughtfully incorporating contingency as an important modus operandi in his work. In other words, Motherwell was able to utilize the ideas of one of the most complex thinkers of the first half of the twentieth century in order to understand art as a non-hierarchical and highly contingent project of self-generating feelings joining him with his media.

Whitehead's process philosophy thus reverses the preeminent role artists have traditionally been accorded in the generation and creation of their work as well as in the development of abstract expressionist art. According to Whitehead, thinking includes humans in processes that incorporate them on an equal footing with elements in the world. In his philosophy, creation is the supra-personal and completely immanent process of "bringing novelty into being."²⁶ For Motherwell, this immanence meant thinking in terms of his artistic media, and conversely allowing his materials to think for and with him. Thus, human thought does not remain isolated at the top of the world's summit; instead, it is immersed in life as an integral part of it. In this way,

Whitehead's metaphysics replaces a human-centered universe with spontaneously self-generated alliances that may be biological or physical as well as both. The resultant entities he describes are not the sole creations of human protagonists, because humans themselves are called forth as part of an ongoing process that involves them as components in temporary or longer-term alliances.

Establishing parity in the act of creation between artist and materials as well as between the creative process and the resultant work of art is the single most important generative concept for Motherwell's overriding collage aesthetic, which he regarded as modern art's single greatest contribution,[27] which in turn informs his paintings, even though he considered painting to constitute a daunting undertaking while collage became a pleasurable one. As comparative literary specialist Mary Ann Caws eloquently points out, "Into his [Motherwell's] collages there could be a great inpouring: everything could have a place, whether inner and outer, whether autobiographical or third-person narrative."[28] Both Motherwell's collages and paintings are predicated on assemblies of different components in order to build diverse types of rhythmic structures in his art.

Motherwell first began making collages in 1943 when Peggy Guggenheim offered him the opportunity to participate in the first international exhibition of this medium to be held in the United States—and he continued to be intrigued with this process to the end of his life. In 1943 and 1944, during his formative years as an artist, Motherwell was primarily involved in experimenting with the collage medium. Several years later he described collages, with their disparate elements, as "relational structures" in which one is symbolically and literally readjusting actual fragments of the world:

> The sensation of physically operating on the world is very strong in the medium of the papier collé or collage, in which various kinds of paper are pasted to the canvas. One cuts and chooses and shifts and pastes, and sometimes tears off and begins again. In any case, shaping and arranging such a relational structure obliterates the need and often the awareness of representation. Without reference to likenesses, it possesses feeling because all the decisions in regard to it are ultimately made on the ground of feeling.[29]

This type of art can be understood as being so fundamental to Motherwell's overall oeuvre that one can view it as subsuming his paintings under its very generous auspices, including even his series of *Elegies to the Spanish Republic*, since his finished canvases, like his collages, are similarly predicated on constellations of flat elements, notable for their organically shaped silhouettes. Regarding the object-like character of his use of paint, Motherwell has stated:

> I think of color as a thing, not as an abstraction. I do not draw shapes and then color them blue; I take a piece of blue, a large extension of blue and cut out, so to speak, from the extension of blue as much blue as I want. Color is a thing for me.[30]

Even though Motherwell had tried over the years to discern fundamental differences between his collages and his paintings, the overall similarities of his approach to the two genres militate against a drastic separation. The main difference between Motherwell's approach to his collages and his painting is the addition of concrete elements from the world of popular culture in the former, such as wrapping paper, maps, cigarette and food wrappers, and various types of packaging sent to the artist as well as the printed materials he finds of interest, making them enormously accessible in their embrace of both high- and low-brow ephemera, while his paintings uphold more directly the high-art standards of modern abstract art. His generous incorporation of aspects of his personal world, such as the cigarettes he smoked or the type of French crackers he ate, is based on an assumption, similar to Jean-Paul Sartre's, that whatever pertains to him is of universal human interest and will prove intriguing and useful. Because these elements, however modest, are joined together in dynamically calibrated, artful arrangements bespeaking a range of vital rhythms, testifying to the artist's sophisticated knowledge of modern art, the ensuing contradictions between materials and means are an updating of an early twentieth-century approach that worked well for the cubists and dadaists. When thinking of Motherwell's painting as extensions of his collage aesthetic, one needs to keep in mind his view that painting also connects his work with the outside world. "For me," he mused in 1947, "the medium of oil painting resists, more strongly than others, content cut off from external relations. It continually threatens, because of its motility and subtlety, to complicate a work beyond the simplicity inherent in a high order of abstraction."[31] In addition to his respect for collage as a visual medium, Motherwell found it to be an important generative concept for one of his long-term favored authors, James Joyce, particularly his *Ulysses*.[32]

Rather than focusing on individual collages or paintings in order to enumerate their different elements and thus arrive at specific iconographic readings—a useful approach found in much of the recently published literature on these works, but also a risky venture since important works of art provide the basis for so many different relevant, yet competing perspectives—my analysis will consider some of Motherwell's collages as well as a few of his paintings more broadly and theoretically in order to appreciate how they work with and even advance specific tenets of Whitehead's process philosophy and related ideas, even though they admittedly often do include specific iconographic references. One of my goals is to think about Motherwell's collage aesthetic more generally by analyzing how it functions interactively to become a remarkable allegory of both art and life. In order to carry out this type of analysis, I will look at a few of these works and their aesthetic realizations as instantiations of a Whiteheadian type of process, comprised not so much of mere things but of the energies they bespeak and the ensuing dynamic relationships they entail. As Whiteheadian works, Motherwell's collages and paintings invite viewers to take part in a contrapuntal activity as well as an ongoing becoming by collaborating with the many semiotic references these works address and the different forces they embody. In order to comprehend the connections between Motherwell's collage aesthetic and Whitehead's process philosophy, I will begin Chapter 2 by looking at this thinker's preeminent reputation and Motherwell's relationship to him in the late 1930s before considering in Chapter 3 the ways Whitehead rethinks philosophy as being on a par with poetry and similarly involved in life's eminently creative, perpetually dynamic, and steadfastly ongoing processes.

Notes

1 An in-depth analysis of the steps Whitehead took in the 1920s to formulate and further explore the basis of his process metaphysics and its ramifications, starting with *Science and the Modern World* and ending with *Process and Reality*, is Lewis S. Ford, *The Emergence of Whitehead's Metaphysics 1925–1929*, "SUNY Series in Philosophy," ed. Robert C. Neville (Albany: State University of New York Press, 1984).

2 Although Whitehead referred to his process philosophy as an organism, I will mostly be using the term process philosophy for his work, as it is the one most often employed when discussing his theories
   Process philosophy has had a long and impressive ancestry as an alternative to substance metaphysics. Its sources can be located in both Eastern and Western thought, and its Western beginnings are attributable to the sixth century B.C.E. Greek thinker Heraclitus of Ephesus. After a long hiatus in which the materialist approach of such a philosopher as Aristotle had been in the hegemony, processist thinking once again took hold, beginning with the late-eighteenth- and early-nineteenth German idealists, followed by such a major figure as Charles S. Peirce and then by Henri Bergson, William James, John Dewey, and, of course, Whitehead.

3 Barbaralee Diamonstein, "An Interview with Robert Motherwell" in H.H. Arnason, ed., *Robert Motherwell*, 2nd ed., new and revised (New York: Harry N. Abrams, 1982), p. 228.

4 Art historian and critic Dore Ashton, who has curated two Motherwell retrospectives in Mexico and in Spain, respectively, in addition to writing extensively about his work and editing the Documents of Modern Art edition of his writings for the University of California Press, has pointed to Whitehead as "one of his

[Motherwell's] most enduring seminal intellectual influences…whose wisdom he retrieves throughout his life in his conversations and writings." Dore Ashton and Joan Banach, eds. *The Writings of Robert Motherwell* (Berkeley, Los Angeles, and London: University of California Press, 2007).

5 According to Stephanie Terenzio, who worked closely with Motherwell when she was editing an anthology of his writings, Matta first introduced Motherwell to psychic automatism in 1941 when the two were in Taxco, Mexico. Terenzio reinforces Motherwell's subscription to this creative practice throughout his life. Stephanie Terenzio, ed., *The Collected Writings of Robert Motherwell* (New York and Oxford: Oxford University Press, 1992), pp. 4 and 15.

6 Theodore Spencer, who attended these affairs in the later 1920s, recounted them 20 years later:

> The [Whiteheads'] apartment rooms on Memorial Drive in Cambridge, Massachusetts, were crowded with students and a few colleagues; in one room there was a circle around Mr. Whitehead, in another there was a circle around his wife. The students were not picked according to their ability nor were they confined to students of philosophy; there were about fifty or sixty of them, men and women, some of them obviously lame ducks, some silent, some over-talkative, but all apparently, of equal interest to the Whiteheads, each optimistically seen as possibly of promise and possibly of good.
>
> Mr. Whitehead sat in an armchair, short and a little bent, dressed in an old-fashioned, almost Victorian style, with a stiff collar, a beautifully tied gray silk four-in-hand, stiff cuffs showing slightly beyond the sleeves of his cutaway…his deep-set blue eyes were wonderfully alive. They beamed and twinkled, not merely because he seemed to like the people he was talking to, but because, one felt, they were reflecting his own pleasure in expressing his thoughts, in relating the subject of the conversation to the deep values, the long-matured and organic vision, within.

Theodore Spencer, "Alfred North Whitehead," *American Scholar* 16, No. 1 (Winter 1946–1947): 84.

7 Alfred North Whitehead, *Modes of Thought* (New York: The Free Press, 1966), p. vii.

8 Paul Cummings, Oral History Interview with Robert Motherwell, Greenwich, CT, November 24, 1971, Archives of American Art, Smithsonian Institution, n.p.

9 Henri Bergson, "An Introduction to Metaphysics," trans. T.E. Hulme (Indianapolis: Hackett Pub Co Inc, 1999), p. 14.

10 In *Adventures in Ideas*, Whitehead devotes chapters to the topics of "Beauty" and "Truth and Beauty," respectively. In them he underscores the fundamental role that beauty, harmony, and thus aesthetics assume in his metaphysics. Alfred North Whitehead, *Adventures of Ideas* (New York and London: Free Press, Macmillan Company, 1933; rpt. Free Press Paperback Edition, 1967), pp. 252–272.

11 *Science and the Modern World*, Lowell Lectures (1925) (London: Macmillan Company, 1925; rpt. New York, Simon & Schuster Inc., Free Press, 1967), p. 87.

12 Alfred North Whitehead, *Religion in the Making* (New York: The Macmillan Co., 1926), p. 104ff.

13 Robert Motherwell, "On Not Becoming an Academic," (1986) paper presented for the panel entitled "Tradition and Innovation: The Realms of Scholarship,"

Harvard University's 350th anniversary celebration, 4 September 1986. Ashton and Banach, eds., *The Writings of Robert Motherwell*, p. 344.

14   Motherwell, "On Not Becoming an Academic" in Ashton and Banach, eds., *The Writings of Robert Motherwell*, p. 344.

15   Tim Clifford, "Chronology" in Jack Flam, Katy Rogers, and Tim Clifford, eds., *Robert Motherwell Paintings and Collages: A Catalogue Raisonné, 1941–1991* Volume 1 (New Haven and London: Yale University Press, 2012), p. 181. Clifford's fine and carefully researched "Chronology" as well as the important and very worthwhile essays by Flam and Rogers in this volume of the Motherwell catalogue raisonné are important starting points for scholars wishing to research work by this artist. My sincere thanks to the authors and the Dedalus Foundation for this enormously useful publication, which profoundly changes the way Motherwell's work can be approached and studied.

16   Martica Sawin, Email to Author, 15 November 2018. Sawin, a respected art critic and art historian, notes, "Meyer Schapiro had recommended Susanne Langer's *Philosophy in a New Key* to my husband, and we both read it." She remembers that other graduate art students were also reading this book.

17   Motherwell credits Matta with separately indoctrinating Arshile Gorky into the merits of psychic automatism. Diamonstein, "An Interview with Robert Motherwell" in Arnason, *Robert Motherwell*, p. 228.

18   The term "palace coup" is one that Motherwell used often in describing his, Matta's, and Baziotes's efforts to form an American group of artists who planned to rebel in the early 1940s against the surrealists living in New York by going back to this style's original tenets. Robert Motherwell, "Interview with Sidney Simon: 'Concerning the Beginnings of the New York School: 1939–1943'" (January, 1967) in Robert Motherwell, "'On Not Becoming an Academic'" in Terenzio, ed., *The Collected Writings of Robert Motherwell*, p. 161.

19   In social situations Motherwell communicated his theory of plastic automatism to Lee Krasner, who was then living with Pollock.

20   Whitehead discusses this idea in his books *Science and the Modern World*, p. 35, and *Process and Reality: An Essay in Cosmology*, eds. David Ray Griffin and Donald W. Sherburne, Corrected Edition, Gifford Lectures (New York: Free Press, 1978), p. 309.

21   Whitehead, *Science and the Modern World*, p. 34.

22   Michael Epperson, "The Correlation of Quantum Mechanics and Whitehead's Philosophy" in *Quantum Mechanics and the Philosophy of Alfred North Whitehead* (New York: Fordham University Press, 2004), p. 124.
      The best sources for Whitehead's thinking about quantum theory are his *Science and the Modern World* and *Process and Reality*.

23   Although Whitehead initially took issue with Albert Einstein's Theory of Relativity by developing a competing theory, he stopped focusing on his approach and offered in *Process and Reality* (1929) his interpretation of Einstein's by then well regarded hypothesis.

24   In *Adventures in Ideas*, Whitehead finds Aristotle responsible for "the static fallacy…which has infected all subsequent philosophy" and condemns John Locke for his "metaphor of the mind as an 'empty cabinet'" since this trope moved existence away from the actualities of "process" by making human reality's "static recipient[s]." Whitehead, *Adventures of Ideas*, p. 276.

25   "Letter from Robert Motherwell to Frank O'Hara" (August 18, 1965) in Terenzio, ed., *The Collected Writings of Robert Motherwell*, p. 148.

26 Ford, *The Emergence of Whitehead's Metaphysics 1925–1929*, p. 127.
27 Letter from Robert Motherwell to Guy Scarpetta, 8 June 1981 in Terenzio, ed., *The Collected Writings of Robert Motherwell*, p. 244.
28 Mary Ann Caws, *Robert Motherwell with Pen and Brush* (London: Reaktion Books, Ltd, 2003), p. 166.
29 Robert Motherwell, "Beyond the Aesthetic," *Design* 47, No. 8 (April 1946): 14. Ashton and Banach, eds., *The Writings of Robert Motherwell*, p. 54.
30 Robert Motherwell, "Interview with Bryan Robertson, Addenda 1965" in Terenzio, ed., *The Collected Writings of Robert Motherwell*, p. 143.
31 Robert Motherwell, "Letter to Samuel Kootz" (21 January 1947) in Terenzio, ed., *The Collected Writings of Robert Motherwell*, p. 43.
32 Joyce continued to be an author of immense significance for Motherwell. For several decades he participated in an ongoing poker game with several psychoanalysts, all dedicated to sharing their own interpretations of Joyce's references, when they were summering in Provincetown, Massachusetts. In June 1975, Motherwell invited me to be an onlooker at one of these poker nights, and the conversation that evening turned as usual to the men's dual games of poker and figuring out certain passages in *Ulysses*.

2 Robert Motherwell, Harvard, and Alfred North Whitehead

Before his death in 1947, Alfred North Whitehead was considered by some to be the "greatest living philosopher."[1] This coveted laurel was based first on his work coauthoring with his former Cambridge University graduate student Bertrand Russell the formidable three-volume *Principia Mathematica* (1910, 1912, and 1913), an acclaimed milestone, which set out to prove that all mathematical truth can be reduced to logic and thus became foundational for the development of symbolic logic. This superlative for Whitehead's philosophy was predicated also on his later serious doubts about *Principia Mathematica*'s premises, leading him to conclude that this exhaustive study constituted a tremendous slip-up. The cumulative effect of this drastic reversal, no doubt an initially painful one to undertake, was Whitehead's embarkation on the entirely new goal of originating in his sixties (that is, the mid-1920s) the twentieth-century type of process metaphysics he called organism, which is usually referred to simply as process philosophy. This term has mainly been associated with Whitehead and theorist Charles Hartshorne, who regarded Whitehead as one of his chief influences. This innovative set of theories depends on a number of antecedents, some going back to antiquity; others are indebted to nineteenth-century innovative studies of cells and to Charles Darwin's theory of natural selection as a reasoned account of endurance and change, and still others are predicated on quantum mechanics in order to theorize an essential dynamism as the ultimate reality, thereby replacing confidence in static matter, which had been a philosophic cornerstone since Aristotle. Determining the limits of scientific materialism as well as advancing the need for the humanities to take into consideration the new physics' advances, Whitehead predicts in *Science and the Modern World*, "The old foundations of scientific thought are becoming unintelligible," before adding, "Time, space, matter, material, ether, electricity, mechanism, organism, configuration, structure, pattern, function, all require reinterpretation," thereby acknowledging the importance of "different notions of temporality."[2] In undertaking this reevaluation, Whitehead became one of the first twentieth-century philosophers to attempt a reconciliation of postclassical physics with humanistic views. In *Modes of Thought*, he writes, "The modern point of view is expressed in terms of energy, activity, and the vibratory differentiations of space-time."[3]

Although Whitehead's ideas, as we will see, were crucial for Motherwell's collage aesthetic, even providing him with a rationale for becoming an artist, since this processist thinker viewed art as being on a par with philosophy, Whitehead had decided to retire from teaching in the spring of 1937, prior to the fall when Motherwell entered Harvard University's graduate program in philosophy. Instead of being able to take classes with Whitehead, Motherwell enrolled in a seminar on Spinoza's ethics and was also permitted to engage in an independent study course on aesthetics with the much younger professor David White Prall (usually abbreviated to D.W. Prall), who served as his advisor and became a close friend and advocate. In the spring semester he enrolled in an independent study course in aesthetics with Prall.[4]

In addition to ongoing conversations with him, Motherwell studied Prall's essentially mainstream formalist texts *Aesthetic Analysis* and *Aesthetic Judgment*. The most important one for Motherwell, *Aesthetic Analysis*, published the year before he met Prall,[5] provides an overview of this thinker's basic ideas that join aspects of the contemporaneous New Criticism (the view that all meanings are to be found in the work of art per se) with an art-for-art's sake formalism, both interpretative theories being predicated on stable works of art—views far removed from the inherent dynamism of Whitehead's philosophy.

In *Aesthetic Analysis* Prall associates the aesthetic realm with the immediate perception of an artwork's sensuous surface and confines meaning to its abstract formal relations. For him the realm of the aesthetic is the experienced surface or skin of the world, which he distinguishes as "the whole world as directly felt"[6] by an artist. Because the work of art distills only the aesthetic skin of the world, Prall believes the artistic experience to consist solely of the immediate apprehension of the work's surface as it is being presented to the viewer.[7] When percipients go beyond the work of art for something not immediately there, they have advanced beyond the realm of the aesthetic—a fixed absolute—and their activities are intellectual, not aesthetic. In order to experience the aesthetic, observers must give their total attention to the qualitative presentation and its given character, even though Prall recognizes that no experience of art can be completely aesthetic or completely lacking in aesthetic character. Despite its inevitable lack of purity, since art is always implicated in the world in which it was created, art, according to Prall, must strive to distill aspects of the world and become an extreme form of abstraction, which can be interpreted as stylization, if it is ever to attain a qualitative distinction. Abstraction is therefore a distillation of the richness and complexity of the everyday world, which, as Socrates's Crytallus dialogue on language's necessary concision teaches, would be overwhelming if its contents were not strictly limited so that one might study and understand them. "Attention," Prall notes, is therefore "directed not only by some interest, but by means of some sort of conceptual scheme" in order to concentrate on "the non-separable but distinguishable aspects of objects."[8] Because Prall's ideas were very much in sync with New Criticism's empirical-based view of works of art as autonomous and static objects dominating aesthetic experience and superintending interpretations of them, his teaching enabled Motherwell to bring his understanding of art to the level of the then-established views of principled formalism but not to go beyond them.

Prall did, however, point Motherwell in the direction of two of his colleagues, Whitehead and Arthur O. Lovejoy. Prall directs attention to Whitehead when he describes the artwork's "emotional character, its *feeling*, that is the way it feels to us…[being] no less genuinely 'objective' than its colors or its sounds, its shapes, its hardness, its presented spread and size."[9] It is as if Prall had picked up certain ideas from Whitehead and was able to affirm their significance for art without being able to explain why. An example of Prall's validation of Whitehead's approach is the following discussion of feeling in art:

> If it is asked how qualitative imaginal content can present feeling, how it can be actual feeling that art expresses, we arrive at the supposed miracle that art is so often said to be, the embodiment of spirit in matter. But thinking can have no intercourse with miracles. And since the simplest thinking finds that works of art do express feelings, we are forced by the obvious character of our data to look for feeling *within* presented content, as an aspect of it, that is, integral to its actually present character, or as its unitary qualitative nature as a whole.[10]

In order to move from this stated truth to its analysis, Motherwell needed first to rethink the dynamic possibilities of romanticism that Lovejoy was able to convey before embarking on Whitehead's far more radical understanding of the world as comprised not of objects but of dynamic vectors of energy. While this learning would ideally occur in several discrete steps, Motherwell was presented with these approaches all at once in the course of his extraordinarily intense academic year at Harvard.

Even though Motherwell worked with Lovejoy[11] and became involved in writing an M.A. thesis on Delacroix under the joint direction of Lovejoy and Prall, Lovejoy's interdisciplinary linked successions of unit ideas over centuries and even millennia could not compete with the intrinsic evolution of energy Whitehead called feelings, which are poised at the very center of the world's perpetual dynamism. Moreover, as important as Lovejoy's exegesis of romanticism as a trajectory focused on completing all possible types of human yearning has become in the twenty-first century's focus on diversity, it could not then compete with Whitehead's view of the sensate basis of the universe encompassing both animate and inanimate forms and his reinterpretation of feelings in terms of a perpetual dynamics of becoming. Rather than looking at feelings as subjective ways of encountering the world, as the romantics had when privileging their own intransigent, colonizing subjectivities, Whitehead's theories enabled Motherwell to conceptualize feelings as existence itself and to understand how they encompassed not only the physical and biological sciences but also the humanities.

Fortunately, although he could not take classes with Whitehead, Motherwell found that the retired professor remained a Harvard institution,[12] even though he was then in his mid-seventies. Whitehead's former colleagues and students still respected his work and enjoyed his wit, and he remained known for the generous hospitality he and his wife extended one night each week to as many as 60 students at each gathering. Whitehead's former student Lucien Price documented these and other events in the delightful book *Dialogues of Alfred North Whitehead*, calling these evenings, which Motherwell no doubt attended, since Harvard students, their special friends and others were welcomed, "a salon in the eighteenth-century French meaning of that term, brought off in an academic town with young men and women on cookies and hot chocolate."[13]

Reflecting in 1971 on his own time at Harvard, when art specialist Paul Cummings interviewed him for the Archives of American Art, Motherwell concluded,

> But probably the main influence was Whitehead, who…was still lecturing at Wellesley where I heard some of the lectures and who was around Harvard all the time. And many of the graduate assistants, etc. were filled with him, and I knew him, so that even though he wasn't literally teaching, his influence was everywhere there.[14]

The Wellesley reference is to the six lectures Whitehead delivered at this institution in 1937–1938, which served as the main focus for *Modes of Thought* (1938), one of the most accessible publications by a man often referred to as among the most difficult of twentieth-century thinkers. Together with these lectures, the insights he gleaned from fellow graduate students who had taken classes with Whitehead, his own acquaintance with the man, and his concerted study of several of his publications, Motherwell was able to gain considerable understanding of his thought.

Like his maternal Irish grandfather, Sean Hogan, an attorney and an amateur intellectual, who built an impressive library containing the complete works of such writers as Darwin, Dostoevsky, Turgenev, and others,[15] Motherwell would amass an impressive number of volumes on a subject of interest and then read them. A distinct boon to his quest to understand Whitehead's ideas is Motherwell's lifelong passion for reading. "I've always been very thorough," he said in his interview with Cummings, "For example, if I decided to read Greek tragedy, I would read all the thirty-seven, or whatever it is, known Greek tragedies. Or if I decided to read André Gide, I would read his complete works. Or Freud. Or Elizabethan drama."[16] However indefatigable Motherwell proved to be in his intellectual pursuits, he also knew how to skim effectively, so he could quickly go through astonishing amounts of material and still be able to discuss it intelligently. But because Whitehead's style of writing resists this summary approach, demanding instead a painfully slow unpacking of dense ideas tied to a highly specialized vocabulary, his work presented Motherwell with enormous challenges.

Far less daunting for Motherwell was the clear prose of John Dewey, whose reputation in the 1920s and 1930s far outdistanced Whitehead's. Since Motherwell had been captivated by Dewey's *Art as Experience* during his undergraduate days at Stanford, his subsequent turn at Harvard to Whitehead's work demands explanation, especially since he later admitted, "I owe Dewey part of my sense of process. He demonstrated philosophically that abstract rhythms, immediately felt, could be an expression of the inner self."[17] Art historian Robert Saltonstall Mattison has beautifully summed up the move by pointing out, "Whitehead completed and enlarged the ideas which Motherwell had already absorbed from Dewey.[18]

One of the single most significant differences between the two philosophers is Dewey's pragmatic insistence on humans as the primary agents responsible for process-based topics and their interpretation, an approach Whitehead undermines. In *Process and Reality*, the essential source for his metaphysical processist views, Whitehead suggests how this position can be overturned. Whitehead states: "Descartes in his own philosophy of organism, conceives the thinker as creating the occasional thought. The philosophy of organism [again, Whitehead's term for process philosophy] inverts the order, and conceives the thought as a constituent operation in the creation of the occasional thinker. The thinker is the final end whereby there is the thought. In this inversion we have the final contrast between a philosophy of substance and a philosophy of organism."[19] As Whitehead concludes, "In the philosophy of organism it is not 'substance' which is permanent, but 'form,' which is in a continual, self-generating "process of becoming."[20] By continuing to rely on human agency, Dewey does not go nearly as far as Whitehead in replacing both a human-centered world and static substances with spontaneously created, mutually dependent alliances that are responsive to rather than responsible for being.[21]

According to Whitehead, then, the impetus for the self-creating and self-determining *event* (defined as a collection or nexus of entities)[22] comes first, and the players, both human and otherwise, are called forth as part of it, so that all entities are complexes—occasions of experience—and thus must be understood as being fully immersed in the world. Whitehead's diachronic structuralism—admittedly a contradiction in terms—is a highly sophisticated means for viewing all the participants in a given process as resulting from it, without any outside agent, including humans, assuming the traditional deus ex machina role of constituting the main determining force. As we will see, this concept is most important for Motherwell's reconceptualizing and consequent deposing the traditional view of the romantic author as the autonomous creator of his or her universe as well as the surrealist idea of psychic automatism as driven by specific individuals. He does so by rethinking the generation of works of art so that they are no longer the creations of isolated subjects but are spontaneously created by collaborating and self-selecting actors (human and otherwise) fully immersed in the world before congregating their antecedent forms as they tacitly agree to become part of a new actual entity. Rather than being created *ex nihilo*, the process is fully *in media res*. Both this spontaneous and serendipitous formation works especially well with the readily available collage materials that are part of Motherwell's everyday world and with the concomitant idea that paintings are assemblies of painted objects.

Although Whitehead never developed a concerted rationale for either looking at art or thinking about it and consequently has not been considered an important figure in aesthetics, his entire system is predicated on a foundation of feelings and creativity, which he views as integral to process philosophy's essential dynamics. As he once said, "Philosophy at its greatest is poetry, and necessitates aesthetic apprehension."[23] On another occasion he equated style with a moral life. "Style in its finest sense," he wrote "is the last acquirement of the educated mind; it is also the most useful. It pervades the whole being…. Style is the ultimate morality of mind."[24] Even though Whitehead defined the process as metaphysical, he began regarding it in the 1920s as being speculative in its "endeavor to frame a coherent, logical, necessary system of general ideas in terms of which every element of experience can be interpreted,"[25] Thus, his response to philosophy is in many respects an aesthetic one.[26] It is predicated on viewing philosophy at times as a way to transpose art's profound insights into rational prose and at other times as a means for arriving at art's own intuitive perceptions into the quality and disposition of reality and its concomitant abstractions of nature in doing so. This twofold view of philosophy as a method for rationally comprehending art's profundity and as itself a route to intuitive grasps of reality's qualitative secrets had an enormous impact on Motherwell's thinking about both philosophy and art, since these two subjects were of the greatest interest to him and appeared in Whitehead's theory to be twin paths to arriving at the same type of vital contents. No doubt the experience of hearing Whitehead expound on them in his Wellesley lectures made philosophy's role as a creative endeavor even more persuasive.

At the beginning and end of *Modes of Thought* Whitehead boldly stated, "philosophy is akin to poetry,"[27] and both endeavors, I would add, in his process metaphysics are inspired conceptions of energy and its ongoing dynamics in the world. Whitehead's analogy between philosophy and poetry is extraordinary for a thinker who had earlier been known for his contributions to analytic philosophy and its overarching logic, even though this approach is anticipated in his opening statement in his well-regarded 1916 address to the Mathematical Association of England. Whitehead begins his speech by asserting, "Culture is activity of thought, and receptiveness to beauty and humane feeling."[28] In *Modes of Thought*, he explained, "Philosophy is the endeavor to find a conventional phraseology for the vivid suggestiveness of the poet." And he elaborates, "It is the endeavor to reduce Milton's "Lycidas" to prose; and thereby to produce a verbal symbolism manageable for use in other connections of thought. "[29]

Whitehead's choice of "Lycidas" in this passage was no doubt a calculated tactic. "Lycides" is a pastoral elegy, written by John Milton in 1637 to memorialize Edward King, who had been his classmate at Cambridge and who had drowned when his ship sank off the coast of Wales. This elegy ends with the death of the allegorical figure, Lycidas, a surrogate for King, at the same time that it reflects on the pastoral world left behind, thereby suggesting that this shepherd's demise is an occasion for a new beginning:

> And now the Sun had stretch'd out all the hills,
> And now was dropt into the Western bay;
> At last he rose, and twitch'd his Mantle blew:
> Tomorrow to fresh Woods, and Pastures new[30]

The empathic characterization of resurrection in these last lines supplies Whitehead with a stirring image that parallels the type of dynamic movement forged by his process philosophy's congregating energies into electromagnetic actual occasions, which are units of creativity, i.e., "conditioned actual entit[ies] of the temporal world."[31] In his system, actual entities are moments of reality, and they are completed before becoming elements in ever-new self-selecting communities of forces culminating in yet other new actual occasions.

The *satisfaction* concomitant with the self-cohering forces making up actual entities (or actual occasions) is Whitehead's standard of beauty, which he defines as "the mutual adaptation of the several factors in an occasion of experience." He then concludes, by pointing out, "Beauty is a quality which finds its exemplification [and its goal] in actual occasions: or put conversely, it is a quality in which such occasions can severally participate."[32] In fact, beauty is so important to Whitehead's metaphysics that he concluded, "The teleology of the Universe is directed to the production of Beauty."[33]

Whitehead's reference to Milton's "Lycidas" also provides the possibility of seeing how this image of death and resurrection correlates with his ideas about feeling or sensing "qualitative energies of the past" so that they might mutually join "into a pattern of qualitative energies in the present occasion"[34] and thus become meaningful symbolic transfers. In *Process and Reality*, Whitehead elaborates on this type of progression. "A feeling appropriates elements of the universe," he writes, " which in themselves are other than the subject, and absorbs these elements into the real internal constitution of its subject by synthesizing them in the unity of an emotional pattern expressive of its own subjectivity." "Feelings," he more simply concludes, "are 'vectors,' for they feel what is *there* and transform it into what is *here*."[35] Even though feelings in the everyday world are usually reserved for characterizations of organic life as one of its prerogatives such as the feelings of humans, animals, and plants, Whitehead views them much more broadly and attributes felt agency to the dynamic situation and not simply to the organic life that might be among its participants.

Although Whitehead did not write specifically about one of his most favored pieces of poetry, William Wordsworth's autobiographical "Prelude," he is known to have enjoyed reading and reflecting on it in his youth and to have continued doing so throughout his life.[36] It proved to be an illuminating resource in his later years, so much so that Victor Lowe, one of his Harvard students who became a specialist in processist theory, was able to conclude, "Wordsworth probably influenced Whitehead as much as any philosopher did, Plato excepted."[37] In *Science and the Modern World*, Whitehead acknowledged, "I hold that the ultimate appeal is to naïve experience and that is why I lay such stress on the *evidence* of poetry."[38] Although Wordsworth's name is not mentioned in this statement, his romantic poetry and quest to recapture his childhood immersion in nature correlates well with the knowing naïveté Whitehead is referencing.

If one wishes to appreciate the type of thinking Whitehead found in Wordsworth's "Prelude," one might begin by considering the following lines from "Book I: Childhood and School-Time":

> That one, the fairest of all Rivers, lov'd
> To blend his murmurs with my Nurse's song,
> And from his alder shades and rocky falls,
> And from his fords and shallows, sent a voice
> That flow'd along my dreams?[39]

My reading of these lines is that nature, personified as a river together with its shades, falls, fords, and shallows, works in tandem with Wordsworth's actual or metaphorical nurse to become part of the poet's own dreams, thereby enacting the collaborative directiveness and enfolding creative unity called the "active Principle"[40] in another of Wordsworth's poems. Elsewhere and on a number of occasions Whitehead refers to this collaborative and self-generated embracing as *ingression* in order to denote the process of self-selecting forces coming together. Whitehead, then, transposes in his theory this "active Principle" into the pulses of experience formative for his processist theory.

In *Science and the Modern World*, Whitehead briefly refers to Wordsworth. "The brooding, immediate presences of things," he explains, "are an obsession to Wordsworth. What the theory [referring to his own maturing views of process philosophy] does is to edge cognitive mentality from its former role as the necessary conductor of unified experience. That unity is now placed in the unity of an event." That unity is what so deeply affected this poet. Then Whitehead dethrones both human mentality and emotions when he adds, "Accompanying this unity [referring to the "brooding immediate presences" and the poet], there may or there may not be cognition,"[41] referring to the traditional central place accorded human understanding.

Creativity, regarded as the ongoing combined drive in the world toward ever-new productions, plays a crucial role in Whitehead's eminently self-motivated process-oriented philosophy. As he succinctly explains, "the whole world conspires to produce a new creation."[42] Because this process necessitates dethroning human beings' formerly preeminent role so that they are integral parts but not the originators or the superintendents of creative developments, I wish to look at the basic orientation of Whitehead's cosmology in which creativity is internal to the ongoing collaborative process of *prehension*, which he sometimes refers to as feeling in order to denote the shared relationship between an entity and its milieu. Prehensions are positive when they permit outside inducements and negative when they preclude them, thereby only positive prehensions can be considered feelings. Prehension is the root word for both apprehension and comprehension. Whitehead uses it to describe the mutual act of spontaneously and noncognitively[43] contributing known contents in self-originating the new beings he calls *actual entities*, which might be anticipated but cannot be known in advance, otherwise they would not represent a new creation. Thus, we can conclude that all prehended (feeling) events are also actual entities.

Whitehead also views prehensions in terms of beauty, to return to a topic discussed earlier; this is a concept that suggests resonances with Motherwell's art. For Whitehead, beauty occurs when prehensions' self-forming components "do not inhibit each other" and when the ensuing "contrasts [between the prehending elements] introduce new conformal intensities of feeling natural to each of them, and by so doing raises the intensities of conformal feeling in the primitive component feelings."[44] Thus, when there is qualitative respect for each of the integral self-congregating components in a culminated actual entity, Whitehead regards this generous alliance as the decisive factor making art feasible.[45]

In *Modes of Thought*, Whitehead analogies prehension and thinking in terms of the ripples in the water in a pond, which are usually caused by a stone thrown in a pool of water. He does so by reversing this scenario so that waves prehensively anticipate the stone's plunge. As Whitehead explains, "A thought is a tremendous mode of excitement. Like a stone thrown into a pond it disturbs the whole surface of our being. But this image is inadequate. For we should conceive the ripples as effective in the creation of the plunge of the stone into the water. The ripples release the thought, and the thought augments and distorts the ripples. In order to understand the essence of thought we must study its relation to the ripples amid which it emerges."[46] Whitehead elaborates on the prehensive process by focusing on actual entities, which he refers to as "the final real things of which the world is made up" and calls them "drops of experience," using William James's expression.[47]

In *Process and Reality*, he connects actual entities and feelings. "Each actual entity" he points out, "is conceived as an act of experience arising out of data. It is a process of "feeling" the many data, so as to absorb them into the unity of one individual "satisfaction." "Here "feeling" is the term used for the basic generic operation of passing from the objectivity of the data to the subjectivity of the actual entity in question. Feelings are variously specialized operations, effecting a transition into subjectivity.... An actual entity is a process, and is not describable in terms of the morphology of a "stuff."[48]

We might more fully appreciate the type of situation Whitehead is describing as an actual entity if we think of the role artists or craftspeople assume when working in clearly defined traditions. If we consider the situation of an Anatolian rug weaver, for example, this individual is integrated into a much larger practice that includes raising sheep, collecting natural and artificial material for dying the wool, working within the sets of traditional designs (constraints) handed down for generations that have been personally inflected but persist in recognizable fashion to be Anatolian. In such a situation the weaver is one component among many. While we might personalize a specific rug weaver's imagination, in the end we can recognize that each constituent—human or otherwise—plays a vital role in an overall governing process that includes the individual weaver as one prehending force (feeling) among a number of other prehending forces. Each plays a vital role in mutually attracting the others, resulting in the actual entity (an individual carpet) that is specific and momentary, even if it survives for centuries. Finally, this carpet represents a variation on the overall Anatolian rug tradition to which it belongs. While this rug is a distinct artifact, Whitehead's philosophy would deemphasize its materiality in favor of the constituting forces coming together to achieve its realization.

In Whitehead's cosmology, the empirical world of prehending elements is balanced by more idealist *eternal objects*, which he defines as "any entity whose conceptual recognition does not involve a necessary reference to any definite actual entities of the temporal world."[49] They exist as "pure potentials," as Whitehead remarks on a number of occasions[50] and are indicative of the Platonic cast of this thought enabling him to account for such generalized qualities as roundness, pointedness, blueness, and bravery. At another time, he concluded, "A colour is eternal. It haunts time like a spirit."[51]

Motherwell understood this difference between generalized colors as eternal objects and specific colors in concrete situations when he pointed out, "The 'pure' red of which certain abstractionist speak does not exist, no matter how one shifts its physical contexts." He continued by saying, "Any red is rooted in blood, glass wine, hunters' caps, and a thousand other concrete phenomena. Otherwise we should have no feeling toward red or its relations, and it would be useless as an artistic element."[52] In this way Motherwell aligns his use of distinct hues like red with the specificity of the components in his collages as well as with Whitehead's actual entities as opposed to eternal objects, i.e., red in potentia. Motherwell's well-known statement about color's specificity is remarkably similar to the following observation by Whitehead: "There is no mere colour, but always some particular colour such as red or blue."[53]

Color, which is a Whiteheadian eternal object when considered generically, is always associative and thus relational when found in a given situation, i.e., when it becomes part of an actual entity, and this is true in even the most abstract works of art. Such positioned colors establish pathways (relations) between their appearance inside works of art and the world outside them. This may be the reason why Motherwell was at great pains in 1950 to connect his predilection for black and white values in his paintings with the chemical origins of black and white paint, the former coming from "charred bones or horns" and "burnt gas," and the latter deriving "from lead," making it "extremely poisonous on contact with the body."[54] Moreover, Motherwell relates white to a distinct literary occurrence, the chapter in *Moby-Dick* entitled "The Whiteness of the Whale," most likely because in his novel Melville aligns whiteness—Whitehead's eternal object and Plato's quality—with an almost mythic albino sperm whale.

Whitehead summarized his overall approach with notable concision when he wrote, "The creativity of the world is the throbbing emotion of the past hurling itself into a new transcendent fact."[55] The "throbbing emotion" in this statement is energy conceptualized as a vector, which Whitehead considers to be an act of working with what is extant to produce a novel result. His anthropomorphization of energy in terms of feelings is difficult to understand until one considers that Whitehead, as noted earlier, does not place humans and their emotions above the rest of the world but instead views all animate and inanimate forms democratically from an atomic point of view. "There is nothing in the real world which is merely an inert fact," Whitehead's proclaims, "Every reality is there for feeling; it promotes feeling; and it is felt."[56] So rocks, mountains, works of art, considered as prehended actual entities, might be regarded as incarnating arrays of feelings or congregations of energetic forces working in tandem.[57] The implicit reference to human subjectivity in Whitehead's above statement is no doubt deliberate because he wishes to highlight an ongoing sensate field of actual entities created through mutual attraction and combined rejection that is taking place atomically and also occurring in larger societies of actual entities. Whitehead's subjective involvement is not consonant with either human or animal consciousness and more often than not operates without it.[58] Considered in this way, Whitehead's actual entities take a "feeling from a beyond which is determinate and… [point] to a beyond which is to be determined," but they are, Whitehead cautions, "subjectively rooted in the immediacy of the present occasion: it is what the occasion [actual entity] feels for itself, as derived from the past and as merging into the future."[59] Never static, actual entities are dynamically shot through with being and becoming, both enjoying the satisfactions of their temporary status, which can last a second, several minutes, many years, and even eons, as these actual entities await the inevitable next stage of becoming raw material for yet other prehensions, then culminating in yet again in newer actual entities. Significantly, Whitehead's system always presupposes a world in which to act and a universe open to change.

Because prehended elements work in concert by mutually inviting the participation of some components while precluding the involvement of others and by devising ad hoc criteria of values to achieve yet-to-be-realized ideals, Whitehead considers this selective process to be an aesthetic one. He describes it somewhat elliptically as "The pattern of sensa characterizing the object [actual entity]—that is, those sensa in that pattern of contrast—enters also into the subject form of the prehension. Thus art is possible."[60] More directly, he concludes, "Thus,… no entity can be divorced from the notion of creativity. An entity is at least a particular form capable of infusing its own particularity into creativity."[61] Since the quest for new actual entities is always a search for new harmonies, one can consider them aesthetically. Lowe has even gone so far as to outline some of the aesthetic categories whereby one might analyze an actual entity such as "harmony and discord, rhythm, intensity, massive simplicity, narrowness and width, inhibition and contrast."[62]

Thus, as core elements in Whitehead's system, actual entities represent an eminently resourceful progression whereby spontaneously congregated elements prehend (sense and survey) their environs (the datum of preexisting entities) in order to join together those elements necessary for their own self-creation. Whitehead considers that the same development that takes place on the atomic level can also be understood as occurring on the human one as long as one thinks of humanity as being comprised of force fields of energy. In the following statement from *Modes of Thought* the personal pronouns "I" and "my" need to be understood as a society of self-created actual entities and not a human individual orchestrating ego:

> My unity…is my process of shaping this welter of material into a consistent pattern of feelings. The individual enjoyment is what I am in my role of a natural activity, as I shape the activities of the environment into a new creation, which is myself at this moment; and yet, as being myself, it is a continuation of the antecedent world. If we stress the role of the environment, this process is causation. If we stress the role of my immediate pattern of active enjoyment, this process is self-creation.[63]

"Consistent pattern[s] of feelings" is certainly an apt way to discuss not only Whiteheadian creations but also Motherwell's work, as he himself was prone to do on a number of occasions throughout his mature life. The legacy of Whitehead's thought was a bequest Motherwell gladly accepted and personalized throughout his life, beginning in the 1940s. As early as 1942, in his "Notes on Mondrian and Chirico," Motherwell stated that it was possible for Mondrian, an expatriate Dutch abstract painter, "to fulfill the artist's function, which is the expression of the felt quality of reality."[64] Although this statement might be taken as just another updating of the traditional view of art as representational, the term "felt quality of reality," in light of Motherwell's study of Whitehead's theories can also be interpreted from a prehensive point of view whereby reality is not a given because it is continually being created and recreated, so that the "felt quality of reality" in a work of art might be construed as an intrinsically new realization and thus a participant in the contrapuntal being/becoming status endemic to Whitehead's process philosophy.

In his lecture for the series of summer talks in Provincetown, Massachusetts, known as Forum 49, named in honor of the year in which they were being presented, Motherwell employed Whitehead's thought as a foundation for his assessment of artistic feelings that he partially conflated with his own, while also paying lip service to Bergson's term "duration":

> form is the emotional unity felt about any object. From this point of view form is subjective feeling; yet is occasioned by an object....Any subject is one by virtue of feeling, anything that feels is for that duration a subject, even if the object of his feeling is his own feeling.[65]

In this same lecture, Motherwell cited the following observation by the German romantic Novalis: "In this state of illusion, it is less the subject who perceives the object than conversely, the objects which come to perceive themselves in the subject." A parallel to this statement comes from the artist's undated notes; it is his observation that "the way to paint a picture is not to paint it, but let it paint you, so to speak."[66] Although this chiastic proposition is weighted in favor of the romantic individual, it can easily be interpreted from the Whiteheadian perspective of congregating prehensive energies. Another of Motherwell's undated notes attributes feelings to the works of art and not the artist: "When the artistic mind is functioning in its medium," he begins, " it is wholly empirical, dominated by structural necessities whose origin is in felt values…art does not have to find good or bad reasons to justify the feeling, art simply expresses the feeling; and the justification is the business of critics."[67]

Although the following statement from 1950 is clearly in sync with Whitehead's approach, it can also be considered an example of Motherwell's reading of Whitehead from a psychological perspective:

> Feeling is the criterion that the painter uses for deciding when a painting is complete—when the feeling is complete so is the painting, using feeling as the basis for establishing the completeness of a painting transfers the decision-making process from a formal to a psychological level.[68]

In this observation Motherwell is notably writing in the third person and transferring agency from the artist to the work of art. This transferal is all-important since it goes against the customary view of abstract expressionist art as an unmediated registration of the artist's innermost self. In terms of this traditional view, the work becomes either a seismograph of the artist's feelings or his or her surrogate.

Also, in 1950 Motherwell devised a more orthodox Whiteheadian approach when he said, "The content of any art is just the world as felt,"[69] meaning it is prehensively culminated in an actual entity at the time of its completion. In 1954 this artist approached prehension both negatively and positively in terms of what it leaves out and also includes. "Abstract art," he opined, "is stripped bare of other things in order to intensify it, its rhythms, spatial intervals, and color structure."[70] Motherwell understood that the artist is only one productive component among others, including his or her chosen media, when he contacted the director of the Blanton Museum of Art at the University of Texas to ask that his 1960 work be listed as *Painting*, rather than *Painter* as the museum had mistakenly assumed. He did so at this time because his emphasis was on the more egalitarian process of making the work and collaborating with his materials rather than isolating himself as its sole creator.[71]

The topic of positive and negative prehensions is crucial to Whitehead's theorization of the autonomous creation of actual entities that necessitate inclusions and exclusions; he regards these value judgments as aesthetic choices that are far removed from mere taste when he attaches moral values to this aesthetic process. In *Religion in the Making* he explicitly states, "the moral order is merely certain aspects of the aesthetic order,"[72] an idea implicit in his discussions of value. In one of his most memorable statements Motherwell picks up on the morality of aesthetic decisions when he writes of ridding his work of outmoded conventions long incorporated in it (negative prehensions) while affirming the feelings it must incarnate (new and positive ones) coming from outside established tradition:

> The struggle has inexorable moral values—no nostalgia, no sentimentalism, no propaganda, no discourse, no autobiography, no violation of the canvas as a surface (since it is one), no clichés, no predetermined endings, no seduction, no charm, no relaxation, no mere taste, no obviousness, no coldness; or, oppositely, for me, it must have immediacy, passion or tenderness; *beingness*, as such, detachment, sheer presence as a modulation of the flat picture plane, true invention and search, light, an unexpected end, mainly warm earth colors and black and white, a certain stalwartness.[73]

While these prehensive rejections and acceptances might appear to constitute a straightforward set of decisions that come before actually making a work of art, as an abstract expressionist Motherwell embraces the additional challenge of finding ways for aspects of the process itself to be revealed in the completed work. Consequently, the pentimenti, gunky painted surfaces implying layers of thought brought together in his art, with the concomitant changes that heralded them, including the seeming tentativeness of bluntly cut and painted edges, as well as the many ripped pieces of paper in his collages, all point to the machinations of an informed prehensive aesthetics. While Motherwell may bemoan the despair of the aesthetic and invoke Søren Kierkegaard's philosophy in doing so, his completed work betrays a delight in revealing his many "layers of mistakes," "layers of consciousness, of willing" that bespeak the creative miracle of hard-won insights.[74]

Moving ahead to the 1960s and 1970s, we find Motherwell still cogitating about creation as a prehensive activity. In conversation with the British art critic and curator David Sylvester, he described the type of discoveries his prehensive approach to painting affords. "But certainly implicit partially," he reflected. "is the feeling, not that 'I'm going to paint something I know,' but 'through the act of painting I'm going to find out exactly how I feel,' both generally and about whatever is specific."[75] Near the beginning of the talk entitled "On the Humanism of Abstraction," which Motherwell presented to students and faculty of St. Paul's School in New Hampshire in 1970, he invokes Whitehead's name. Speaking in a manner Whitehead would approve, Motherwell directs his painting away from himself and connects it with the process of making a work of art. "The real subject-matter," he intoned, "is an assumption that what painting is, is the pressure of the brush with a colored liquid on a flat surface." In this same talk, he connects his work with actual entities when he speaks of "states of feeling."[76]

Despite Motherwell's wide-ranging foundation in philosophy and continued interest in the subject, which he embraced throughout his life, Whitehead is the philosopher whom he not only cites far more often than any other thinker but also the theorist whose ideas can be discerned as permeating many of Motherwell's most important views of creativity and feeling—two topics that remained of absorbing interest to him—as I have attempted to demonstrate.

As a codicil to this discussion, I should point out that several theorists have investigated the possibility of reconceiving Whitehead's concepts in terms of aesthetics. Cultural theorist Steven Shaviro views the formation of actual entities as aesthetically shaped objects. "The crucial point," he writes, "is that the same movement that transforms an affective encounter into an objectively cognizable state of affairs also, and simultaneously, offers up that state of affairs as an object for aesthetic contemplation."[77]

In *A Whiteheadian Aesthetic*, philosopher Donald W. Sherburne theorizes a way to move from Whitehead's creative world to an aesthetic one by building on his description of self-creation in *Process and Reality*:

> The "subjective aim," which controls the becoming of a subject is that subject feeling a proposition with the subjective form of purpose to realize it in that process of self-creation.[78]

Central to this definition is Whitehead's insight into a proposition as "a coupling of the concrete and the abstract," which Sherburne explains is "a special type of integration synthesizing a physical feeling with a conceptual feeling."[79] When Sherburne then asserts that "a work of art has the ontological status of a Whiteheadian proposition," an actual entity, he is emphasizing the combination of these two types of feeling, which he interprets as a "lure" for future percipients, who (again feel) the proposition's contents aesthetically, according to their own experiences and dispositions.[80] In other words, viewers of works of art join in the collaborative process in which the artwork, their perception and understanding of it, and the circumstances in which it is being seen all come together to form a new actual entity.[81] Instead of regarding interpretation as a superimposition on a work of art by a percipient who might be a general viewer, critic, art historian, or fellow artist, Sherburne considers such a reading to be part of a dynamic combined venture including the given work of art and the viewer's response to it. Together the two forge yet another work of art, this time an actual entity that is highly conceptual since it revolves around an interpretation of the artwork. Although literary theorist N. Katherine Hayles was discussing posthumanism and ecology in the following statement, her remarks are apposite for Sherburne's theory and help to clarify it, especially if we substitute art network for system:

> [A]s soon as you begin to envision the human actor as a component of a large and complex system [art network] with other agents also at work within that system [art network], there's an inevitable tendency to de-centre the human subject, and then, in second-order cybernetics, to realize more fully that even the place of the observer in such a system [art network] has implications, with the system [art network] capturing and affecting the observer even as the observer tries to position himself outside the system.[82]

Notes

1 Edmund T. Whittaker, "Alfred North Whitehead (1861–1947)," *Obituary Notices of Fellows of the Royal Society* 6, No. 17 (November, 1948): 280–296.

2 Alfred North Whitehead, *Science and the Modern World*, pp. 16 and 118.

3 Whitehead, *Modes of Thought*, p. 138.

4 Clifford points out that Motherwell became part of a small coterie of graduate students who would meet informally with Prall. They included Arthur Berger, who became a noted composer and music critic; Leonard Bernstein, who also became a composer as well as conductor and author; Harry Levin, who became known for his work as an American literary critic and authority on modernism; and Delmore Schwartz, who established a reputation as a poet and short-story writer. At the time, Prall was highly political: he headed up the Harvard Teacher's Union and was committed to liberal values then under assault by Spanish fascists during the contemporary Spanish Civil War (1936–1939). Clifford, "Chronology" in Flam, Rogers, and Clifford, eds., *Robert Motherwell Paintings and Collages: A Catalogue Raisonné, 1941–1991*, Volume 1, p. 182.

5 D.W. Prall, *Aesthetic Analysis* (New York: Thomas Y. Crowell Co., 1967, rpt. 1936).

6 D.W. Prall, *Aesthetic Analysis*, p. 5.

7 D.W. Prall, *Aesthetic Analysis*, p. 6. The main source for my discussion is Prall's introductory chapter in which he sets out the terms of his theory.

8 D.W. Prall, *Aesthetic Analysis*, pp. 23 and 35.

9 D.W. Prall, *Aesthetic Analysis*, p. 143.

10 D.W. Prall, *Aesthetic Analysis*, p. 145.

11 In addition to working with Prall, Motherwell enrolled in the year-long seminar entitled "The Idea of Romanticism," taught by Arthur O. Lovejoy, a distinguished visiting scholar from Johns Hopkins University. Lovejoy's William James Lectures were presented at Harvard in 1933 and were then published in 1936 under the title *The Great Chain of Being: A Study in the History of an Idea*. This work became the model for scholarship in the history of ideas and was a most useful text for a romanticism seminar. Instead of contenting himself with writing a history of philosophy, Lovejoy looked at the persistence of certain "unit ideas" extending over the millennia from Plato to the late eighteenth- and early nineteenth-century romantics and occurring in the sciences and the arts, particularly in literature. He did so in order to detect their transformations and ways of reemerging. He believed, however, that the different romanticisms occurring in the late eighteenth and early nineteenth centuries represented a decisive break in humankind's view of itself that continued to the present day. Instead of adhering to classical ideals traditionally predicated on original tenets and rules of norm, romantics, according to Lovejoy's *The Great Chain of Being*, replaced the classical principles of perfection and self-sufficiency with the new and dynamic views of a never-to-be-achieved completeness coupled with a daunting plenitude. This change resulted in a new emphasis on utilizing potentials so that all possible types of being might be realized, and novelty and diversity might also be looked on positively, rather than be seen as aberrations diverting from the norm. One important legacy of viewing romanticism as a means for understanding the development of a more comprehensive and inclusive world was the realization that it could never be realized; thus the romantic objective of continual becoming—a heroic striving extending into infinity—was introduced, while the former securities of the classical world's perpetual and unchanging ideal types were left far behind.

"I remember," Motherwell said in reference to Lovejoy's course, "someone took the Schlegel Brothers, someone else Coleridge, someone else perhaps the young Karl Marx, and on learning of my interest in painting, Lovejoy assigned to me *The Journal of Eugène Delacroix*, the great French Romantic painter." [Robert Motherwell, "On Not Becoming an Academic" (1986) in Dore Ashton and Joan Banach, eds., *The Writings of Robert Motherwell*, p. 344.] Walter Pach's translation of Delacroix's *Journal* into English had been published earlier that year, making this artist's work accessible to a much larger audience than before. Because of the quality of Motherwell's research paper on Delacroix, Lovejoy, with Prall's encouragement, urged him to go to France the next year to pursue this topic.

Of particular interest to Motherwell's future development and a factor in his attraction to Whitehead's and Langer's theories is Delacroix's view of painting as a mutually reinforcing arrangement like poetry, which is dependent on all its constituent parts in order to communicate holistically through affiliations called "images," rather than simply and directly in terms of lifelike representations. This reliance on emotional gestalt-like images makes Delacroix an uncharacteristic romantic, since artists of this persuasion usually subscribed to a belief in the direct transcription of feelings. Delacroix's innovative and indirect perspective, in fact, aligns his thought with the twentieth-century approach known as "structuralism," since individual terms in structuralism become meaningful in terms of overarching formations rather than singly and autonomously. "In the artist, imagination does more than picture certain objects to itself," Delacroix explains in the *Journal*. "[I]t combines them for the purpose which he seeks to achieve; imagination gives him images with which he composes at will." [Eugène Delacroix, *The Journal of Eugène Delacroix*, trans. Walter Pach (New York: Crown Publishers, 1937, rpt. 1980), p. 561.] As literary specialist Elizabeth Abel has concluded, "Good painting," for Delacroix, "is not reducible to statement; rather, it expresses and evokes a state of mind indirectly through the interplay of all its parts." [Elizabeth Abel, "Refunding the Sister Arts: Baudelaire's Response to the Art of Delacroix," *Critical Inquiry* 6, No. 3 (Spring, 1980): 372.]

In his 1970 introduction to the Viking Press edition of Delacroix's *Journal*, Motherwell describes the general effect that Delacroix's searching and tentative mind in his *Journal* had on his overall view of modern art:

> The image of Delacroix's alert and cultivated mind constantly rolling, like an ever-changing tide, over the rocky questions of *l'art moderne*...remained a sustaining moral force in my inner life. [Robert Motherwell, "Introduction to the Compass Edition," in *The Journal of Eugène Delacroix*, trans. Walter Pach (New York: Viking Press, 1972), pp. 7–8. Ashton and Banach, eds., *The Writings of Robert Motherwell*, p. 286.]

Unfortunately, neither Motherwell's paper on Delacroix nor his notes and subsequent work on his *Journal* while living in France during 1938–1939 are extant.

12 Joseph Gerhard Brennan, "Teaching: Alfred North Whitehead: Plato's Lost Dialogue," *The American Scholar* 47, No. 4 (Autumn, 1978): 516.

13 Lucien Price, *Dialogues of Alfred North Whitehead, as Recorded by Lucien Price* (New York: New American Library, a Mentor Book, 1956), p. 15.

14 Cummings, Oral History Interview with Robert Motherwell, Greenwich, CT, November 24, 1971, Archives of American Art, Smithsonian Institution, n.p.

15 Paul Cummings, Interview with Robert Motherwell, n.p.

16 Paul Cummings, Interview with Robert Motherwell, n.p.

17 Robert Saltonstall Mattison, *Robert Motherwell: The Formative Years*, Studies in the Fine Arts: The Avant-Garde, No. 56 (Ann Arbor and London: UMI Research, 1987), p. 7.
   Caws repeatedly refers to Dewey and American pragmatism as essential American aspects of Motherwell's thought and art, which she pits against his European affiliations. Caws, *Robert Motherwell with Pen and Brush*.

18 Mattison, *Robert Motherwell: The Formative Years*, p. 11.

19 Whitehead, *Process and Reality: An Essay in Cosmology*, p. 151.

20 Whitehead, *Process and Reality: An Essay in Cosmology*, p. 29.

21 Although Motherwell enrolled in Columbia University's graduate art history program in order to work with Meyer Schapiro, who had been one of Dewey's students, Schapiro had great reservations about the relevance of Dewey's philosophy for the study of art.
   Meyer Schapiro, Lillian Schapiro, and David Craven, "A Series of Interviews" (July 15, 1992–January 22, 1995), *Anthropology and Aesthetics* 31, The Abject (Spring, 1997): 159.

22 Whitehead, *Process and Reality*, p. 80.

23 Whitehead cited in Spencer, "Alfred North Whitehead," p. 84.

24 Whitehead cited in Spencer, "Alfred North Whitehead," p. 82.

25 Whitehead, *Process and Reality*, p. 3.

26 Steven Shaviro, "Pulses of Emotion: Whitehead's "Critique of Pure Feeling," http://www.shaviro.com/Blog/?p=1309, consulted 5 April 2018.
   Shaviro writes:

   More broadly, Whitehead's affect theory places aesthetics—rather than ontology (Heidegger) or ethics (Levinas)—at the center of philosophical inquiry. Aesthetics is the mark of what Whitehead calls our *concern* for the world, and for entities in the world.

   Shaviro's reference to concern calls to mind Whitehead's statement:

   It must be distinctly understood that no prehension, even of bare sensa, can be divested of its affective tone, that is to say, of its character of a 'concern' in the Quaker sense. Concernedness is of the essence of perception.

   Alfred North Whitehead, "Objects and Subjects," *Proceedings and Addresses of the American Philosophical Association* 5 (1931): 135.

27 Whitehead, *Modes of Thought*, pp. vii and 237.

28 Alfred N. Whitehead, "The Aims of Education," Presidential Address to the Mathematical Association of England (1916) in Alfred N. Whitehead, *The Aims of Education and Other Essays* (New York: Free Press, 2011), p. 1.

29 Whitehead, *Modes of Thought*, p. 50.

30 John Milton, "Lycidas" in C.A. Patrides, ed., *Milton's Lycidas: The Tradition and the Poem* (New York: Holt, Rinehart, and Winston, 1961), p. 9.

31   Whitehead, *Process and Reality*, p. 88. Whitehead notes that actual entities include God as a lure while actual occasions do not. Since actual entity is the most used term, I am subscribing to this practice. Also, I am using actual entities and actual occasions interchangeably, as some authors have done, since theological concerns are not part of my investigation.

32   Whitehead, *Adventures of Ideas*, p. 252.

33   Whitehead, *Adventures of Ideas*, p. 265.

34   Whitehead, *Modes of Thought*, p. 165.

35   Whitehead, *Process and Reality*, p. 275.

36   English literature specialist Mary A. Wyman cites A.N. Whitehead's daughter Jessie, who related in November 1953: "He would read *The Prelude* as if it were the Bible, pouring over the meaning of various passages." Mary A. Wyman, "Whitehead's Philosophy of Science in the Light of Wordsworth's Poetry," *Philosophy of Science* 23, No. 4 (October, 1956): 283. In his "Autobiographic Notes," Whitehead recalls that during his teenage years in Sherborne before entering Cambridge in 1880, "Poetry, more especially Wordsworth and Shelley became a major interest, and also history."

   Alfred North Whitehead, "Autobiographical Notes" in Paul Arthur Schilpp, ed., *The Philosophy of Alfred North Whitehead Library of Living Philosophers*, Vol. III (Evanston and Chicago: Northwestern University, 1941), p. 6.

37   In this statement Lowe most likely was underscoring the idea that Whitehead like Plato acknowledges the ultimate power of a universal realm, but Whitehead's view, as we will see, unlike Plato's, is not static; instead it is characterized by unending interplays of forces, signaling the universe's inherent and ongoing creativity. Victor Lowe, "The Philosophy of Whitehead," *Antioch Review* 8, No. 2 (Summer, 1948): 232.

38   Whitehead, *Science and the Modern World*, p. 89.

39   In *Science and the Modern World* (p. 84) Whitehead cites the section of the *Prelude* beginning with "Ye Presences of Nature in the sky/And on the earth!" I have instead selected the beginning of Wordsworth's poem as being particularly representative of Whitehead's thought.

40   William Wordsworth writes in "The Excursion" 9, 1–9 in *William Wordsworth, Poems, Volume Two*, ed. John O. Hayden (London: Penguin, 1977):

> "To every Form of being is assigned,"
> Thus calmly spake the venerable Sage,
> An *active* Principle:--howe'er removed
> From sense and observation, it subsists
> In all things, in all natures; in the stars
> Of azure heaven, the unenduring clouds,
> In flower and tree, in every pebbly stone
> That paves the brooks, the stationary rocks,
> The moving waters, and the invisible air.

41   Whitehead, *Science and the Modern World*, p. 92.

42   Whitehead, *Process and Reality*, p. 99.

43   Regarding the word prehension, Whitehead points out:

The word "perceives" is, in our common usage, shot through and through with the notion of cognitive apprehension. So is the word *apprehension*, even with the adjective *cognitive* omitted. I will use the word *prehension* for uncognitive *apprehension*; by this I mean *apprehension* which may or may not be cognitive.

Whitehead, *Science and the Modern World*, p. 70.

44 Whitehead, *Adventures in Ideas*, p. 252.

45 Whitehead, *Adventures of Ideas*, pp. 253–254.

46 Whitehead, *Modes of Thought*, pp. 50 and 51.

47 Whitehead, *Process and Reality*, p. 18

48 Whitehead, *Process and Reality*, p. 40ff.

49 Whitehead, *Process and Reality*, p. 70.

50 Sydney E. Hooper, "Professor Whitehead's 'Adventures of Ideas,'" *Philosophy* 8, No. 31 (July 1933): 333.

51 Whitehead, *Science and the Modern World*, p. 87.

52 Motherwell, "Beyond the Aesthetic," *Design* 47, No. 8 (April, 1946): 14–15. Ashton and Banach, eds., *The Writings of Robert Motherwell*, p. 55. Caws wisely connects the suggestiveness of Motherwell's color with Stéphane Mallarmé's indirection, which is concerned with the effect an object has on a reader rather than the object per se. She elucidates, "The effect is both multiple and radiant. So that, for example, if he [Motherwell] paints an orange picture, it is not simply pure orange: 'it also has to do with fruit, with the sun, with skin, with lots of things." Caws, *Robert Motherwell with Pen and Brush*, p. 37. Caws is citing Motherwell's addenda to the Museum of Modern Art *Lyric Suite* questionnaire, from *"Memory...with Possible Chronological Slips,"* Fall, 1969.

53 Alfred North Whitehead, *Symbolism: Its Meaning and Effect: Barbour-Page Lectures, University of Virginia* (1927) (New York: Fordham University Press, 1985), p. 35.

54 Robert Motherwell, "Black or White" in *Black or White: Paintings by European and American Artists*, exhibition catalogue (New York: Samuel Kootz Gallery, 1950), n.p. Ashton and Banach, eds., *The Writings of Robert Motherwell*, p. 86.

55 Whitehead, *Adventures of Ideas*, p. 177.

56 Whitehead, *Process and Reality*, p. 310.

57 Because different energies collaborate without being subservient to a human agent, we might be tempted to view Whitehead's approach in terms of deep ecology *avant la lettre*. In 1973 Norwegian philosopher Arne Naess developed in a paper the term deep ecology as a necessary move from traditional instrumental ecological perspectives that viewed balanced natural habitats mainly in terms of their usefulness to human beings.

58 Steven Shaviro, "Whitehead on Feelings," http://www.shaviro.com/Bolg/?p=1309, consulted 5 April 2018.

59 Whitehead, *Process and Reality*, p. 162.

60 Whitehead, *Adventures of Ideas*, p. 216.

61 Whitehead, *Process and Reality*, p. 213.

62 Victor Lowe, *Understanding Whitehead*, p. 248.

63 Whitehead, *Modes of Thought*, p. 166.

64 Robert Motherwell, "Notes on Mondrian and Chirico," *VVV* 1 (June, 1942): 59. Ashton and Banach, *The Writings of Robert Motherwell*, p. 15. Motherwell's piece on Mondrian, his first published article, was both early and prescient, as it was written less than a year after this Dutch artist emigrated to the United States and soon after he had his first one-person exhibition in New York.

65 Robert Motherwell, "French Art vs. U.S. Art Today," Lecture for Forum 49, Provincetown, Massachusetts (11 August 1949). TS, Dedalus Foundation Archives.

66 Robert Motherwell, Unpublished Notes, n.d. Dedalus Foundation Archives.

67 Robert Motherwell, Unpublished Notes, n.d.

68 Robert Motherwell, "Statement," *Fourth Annual University of Illinois Exhibition of Contemporary American Painting* (Urbana: University of Illinois, 1950), n.p. TS, Dedalus Foundation Archives.

69 Robert Motherwell, "The New York School," Lecture to Midwestern College Art Association Conference (1950), TS, Dedalus Foundation Archives.

70 Robert Motherwell, "Statement" in Ralph A. Anderson, Jr., *4 Americans from the Real to the Abstract* (Houston: Contemporary Arts Association, January 10– February 11, 1954).

71 Jack Flam, "Introduction: Robert Motherwell at Work" in Flam, Rogers, and Clifford, eds., *Robert Motherwell Paintings and Collages: A Catalogue Raisonné, 1941–1991* Volume 1 (New Haven and London: Yale University Press, 2012), p. 2.

72 Alfred North Whitehead, *Religion in the Making* (Cleveland: Meridian Books, 1961), p. 101.

73 Robert Motherwell, "A Process of Painting" in *The Creative Use of the Unconscious by the Artist and by the Psychotherapist*, ed. Jules Barron and Renee Nell, *Annals of Psychotherapy: Journals of the American Academy of Psychotherapists*, monograph No. 8, Vol. 5, No. 1 (1964): 49. Ashton and Banach, eds., *The Writings of Robert Motherwell*, p. 216.

74 Max Kozloff, "An Interview with Robert Motherwell: 'How I admire my colleagues,'" *Artforum* 4, No. 1 (September, 1965): 34.

75 David Sylvester, "Painting as Existence," Interview with Robert Motherwell. TS, Dedalus Foundation. The edited video was presented under the more conventional title "Painting as Self-discovery" (London: BBC, 22 Oct. 1960.)

76 Robert Motherwell, "On the Humanism of Abstraction: The Artist Speaks" (1970) in Robert Motherwell at St. Paul's School, exhibition catalogue (Concord, NH: St Paul's School, 1971), pp. 5 and 10–11. Ashton and Banach, eds., *The Writings of Robert Motherwell*, pp. 250 and 253.

77 Steven Shaviro, "Pulses of Emotion: Whitehead's "Critique of Pure Feeling."

78 Donald W. Sherburne, *A Whiteheadian Aesthetic* (New Haven: Yale University Press, 1961, rpt. Archon Books, 1970), p. 143.

79 Whitehead, *Process and Reality*, p. 60 and Sherburne, p. 46.

80 Sherburne, *A Whiteheadian Aesthetic*, p. 124.

81 Lowe writes, "His [Whitehead's] central problem is to convince us that a percipient, in an individual moment of experience directly feels the causal derivation of that experience from an environment of other actualities." Victor Lowe,

"The Influence of Bergson, James and Alexander on Whitehead," *Journal of the History of Ideas* 10, No. 2 (April, 1949): 280.

82 N. Katherine Hayles, "How We became Posthuman: Ten Years On, An Interview with N. Katherine Hayles," *Paragraph* 33, No. 3 "Psychoanalysis and the Posthuman" (November, 2010): 325–326.

3 Motherwell's Whitehead
The Felt Quality of Reality

In his writings and interviews, Motherwell repeatedly asserts that art in itself comprises "states of feeling," qualitatively realized, even as it responds to the contemporaneous felt nature of the world in which it is conceived. "The game," he writes, "is not what things "look like." The game is organizing, as accurately and with as deep discrimination as one can, states of feeling; and states of feeling, when generalized, become questions, of light, color, weight, solidarity, airiness, somberness, heaviness strength, whatever."[1] Motherwell also separates feeling from emotion; he makes notable distinctions between the feelings embodied in works of art and incarnated in the world [Whitehead's prehensions and actual entities] that are opposed to the subjective emotions haunting individuals, causing them to prejudge the world around them. In c.1950 he opined:

> I should like to make a distinction between feeling and emotion.... Feelings...are always "objective," the felt quality of things in perception. A work of art belongs to this world of feeling; its fundamental nature is that of an "object" that is meant to be enjoyable to feel, or, more accurately, is meant to feel, and is consequently enjoyable....Emotion, on the contrary, is not determined by what is immediately surrounding one, but is something already in one, that one carries around with one.[2]

Considered in this manner, feelings are Whiteheadian and are embodied in actual entities and events, while emotions, as individual endorsed and harbored patterns, resist such dynamics.

However, in spite of the clarity of this differentiation between feeling and emotion, Motherwell on occasion mixed the two together with less than ideal results. "The emergence of abstract art," he wrote in his talk in 1951 at the Museum of Modern Art (hereafter MoMA), "is one sign that there are still men able to assert feeling in the world. Men who know how to respect and follow their inner feelings, no matter how irrational or absurd they may first appear."[3] But even with this lapse whereby feeling and emotion are conflated, which would recur on occasion, I believe Motherwell preferred to view the feelings comprising his art in terms of Whitehead's more objective self-generative actual entities and events. This thinking is implicitly evident in his observation: "The subject does not pre-exist. It emerges out of the interaction between the artist and the medium. That is why, and only how a picture can be creative."[4] Another example of Motherwell's continued reliance on feeling is found in his letter to the New York poet and MoMA curator Frank O'Hara, which was published as the artist's statement in the catalogue for Motherwell's 1965 retrospective at this museum. "What better way to spend one's life than to have, as one's primary task, the insistence on integrity of feeling? No wonder others are fascinated by artists."[5] Taking this statement into account with Motherwell's observation, "The function of the artist is to express reality as *felt*,"[6] one can appreciate the uncommon role this artist allocates to feelings, which are far removed from traditional romantic intimations, sentimental views, and individual expressions of emotion, since he regards them, after studying Whitehead, as objective ways of getting in touch with "the final real things of which the world is made,"[7] with, i.e., actual entities. In an interview that took place in 1974, Motherwell described the emotion-feeling polarity in terms of unsuccessful expressionist works versus classical effective ones. "One of my main problems in painting," Motherwell explained, "has been a swinging back and forth from expressionism, which I think is basically (as I've defined the word) an emotional thing, toward a modern classicism, like Miró or Matisse, which I think is a felt thing."[8]

Not surprisingly, when Motherwell originated the name "School of New York" for his art and that of his fellow abstract expressionists in October 1950 for a session at the Mid-Western Conference of the College Art Association entitled "Appraisals of Contemporary Art," he relied on the concept of both artists and their individual works as feeling (prehensive) and self-realizing (conscrescing) actual entities (completed paintings):

> One might say that the School of New York tries to find out what art is precisely through the process of making art. That is to say, one discovers, so to speak, rather than imposes a picture. What constitutes the discovery is the discovery of one's own feeling, which none of us would dare to propose before the act of painting itself.[9]

After making this statement about himself and his fellow abstract expressionists in this essay, Motherwell personalizes it by considering himself and his work in terms of a united actualizing entity: "It is only through the process of making that I really know—if you will excuse me a sloppy idiom—what I feel about the world. The content of any art is just the world as felt."[10] Perhaps Motherwell regards this statement as "sloppy" because it conflates his subjective emotion with the objective feeling of actual entities, "the world as felt."

On several occasions in conversation and in his writings, Motherwell has made direct references to Whitehead; in addition, he has frequently and indirectly cited a number of this thinker's ideas. His direct references have tended to be explanations for how and why he was able to become an abstract painter, without going through a period of making representational work. One of the most concise and informative of Motherwell's analyses of his reasons for becoming an abstract painter occurs in the document called the "Final Page of Letter to Unknown Party, Early 1952," published in *The Collected Writings of Robert Motherwell*, edited by Stephanie Terenzio. Because Motherwell worked closely with Terenzio on this project during the late 1980s and early 1990s, which was then published the year after his death, the title of this fragment and its inclusion in this anthology was no doubt undertaken with his approval and probable encouragement. In this letter Motherwell posits the idea of painting as a relational structure, which I view as a personal updating of Whitehead's prehensive forces. He subscribes to this process thinker's theory about philosophy's ability to elucidate, through logic, contents similar to those found in art. As support for his conclusion that painting is first and foremost comprised of affiliating parts, Motherwell extrapolates from Whitehead in order to make his own observation about how art works,

> I have always assumed that the essential nature of intelligence's functioning is the grasp of relations. Many of the relations that a painter grasps are nonverbal....Yet the relations in painting *are* essentially wordless.[11]

Conceiving abstract art as an assembly of interacting components was critical for Motherwell as early as 1942 when he was comparing Mondrian's art to scientific "relations and abstract relational structure."[12] Eight years later he attributes the concept of using a "separate color as a self-determining relational structure" to Matisse in his introduction to Georges Duthuit's *The Fauvist Painters* (volume 11 in The Document of Modern Art series he was editing) before citing Whitehead a few lines later as key to the idea of achieving such formations through emphasis.[13]

Because the concept of art as a relational structure—again, organizations of prehensive feelings—is crucial for understanding Motherwell's consideration of Whitehead, I would like to emphasize that the main reality in his art, including both collages and paintings, is comparable to quantum physics and the interdependent forces, i.e., energy, between various prehending elements that set in motion their temporal passage—not the participating components per se. In process philosophy these substances are bypassed in order to emphasize various types of occurrences and their means of becoming. Although the materials that are definitely part of Motherwell's collage aesthetic might suggest that his work continues to perpetuate traditional Western metaphysical views of a static world of enduring substances, it actually works in tandem with process philosophy, as I have been proposing. Motherwell's collage aesthetic demotes its detritus from daily life to the role of fragments—even to the point of considering the color blue, in his earlier cited statement, to be a piece of this color—while enlisting his selected components in the far more important goal of creating the types of interactions on which his abstractions are poised. Motherwell, then, enjoins viewers to appreciate his art first in terms of their many different velocities, which can range from the competing, almost warring factions of shapes in his early collages to the subdued, seemingly inexorable tensions of his *Elegies to the Spanish Republic* and the stately conversations between foreground figures and nuanced backgrounds in his *Opens*. Percipients of Motherwell's art are thus encouraged to appreciate the spirited rhythms giving rise to a particular work before concerning themselves with the iconographic references to the outside world these works might suggest.

Motherwell considered sets of relationships, i.e., self-marshaling tensions or prehensive feelings, to be singularly important to him and his work, and he repeated this idea often. One of his most cogent explications can be found in his interview with British critic Bryan Robertson, then curator of London's Whitechapel Art Gallery. Responding to Robertson's question about the role Motherwell's philosophical training played in his awareness of artistic form and its ramifications, the artist summarized his own structuralist approach to painting:

> I have continuously been aware that in painting I am always dealing with—and never not—a relational structure. Which in turn makes "permission" to be "abstract" no problem at all. All paintings are essentially relational structures—whether figuration is present or not is not the real issue. So that I could apprehend, for example, at first sight, my first abstract art....I was able to be an abstract painter right off the bat, if I so chose. Which I did. . . .
>
> I understood, too, that "meaning" was the product of the relations among elements, so that I never had the then common anxiety as to whether an abstract painting had a given meaning....
>
> There is a phrase from Whitehead that was of great help: "The higher the degree of abstraction the lower the degree of complexity."[14]

While Whitehead may have been referring in this statement to eternal objects, such as basic geometric forms, colors in the abstract, and such qualities as roundness, squareness, etc., rather than actual entities accruing specific meanings in individual artworks by being located in given situations, Motherwell's account of the interacting elements in his compositions more closely approximates prehended elements. In other words, as noted earlier, a relational structure is a prehensive assemblage of different self-selected energies forming the unity of Whitehead's actual entity. According to this philosopher:

> Life lies below this grade of mentality. Life is the enjoyment of emotion, derived from the past and aimed at the future. It is the enjoyment of emotion which was then, which is now, and which will be then. This vector character is of the essence of such entertainment.[15]

Whitehead's use of the word "emotion" needs to be understood as "feeling" in both his and Motherwell's lexicon, which I have been discussing. At another time Whitehead describes "vector feeling" in terms of "primitive experience," which is basic or foundational.[16] Rather than focusing on static things and inert substances, Whitehead, as discussed earlier, emphasizes concentrated forces. In doing so, his process philosophy considers the world in terms of momentary or more enduring relationships, briefly constellated forces or vectors, and not objects, which only appear to be made up of matter, but which are in actuality the fleeting or longer lasting assemblages of energy comprising his actual entities.

This emphasis on energy, coupled with Whitehead's reference to "life… below this grade of mentality," might be one of the reasons Motherwell embraced Freud's analyses of drives and instincts as particularly cogent ways of coping with energy generated by the libido[17] and was less engaged with Jung's syntheses of shadowy engendered figures emanating from the unconscious. However, Motherwell did remain throughout his life open to this analytical psychologist's views of archetypes as possible genetic predispositions toward certain universal images and myths, but he continued to preface his remarks about archetypes by starting with the conditional, "if there is such a thing as an archetype."[18] Thus, Motherwell's familiarity with both Whiteheadian process philosophy and Freudian psychology encouraged him to view the world and his art as comprised of ongoing tensions betokening structured forces of energy. One of his most empathic statements on this subject is entitled "Beyond the Aesthetic":

> It is natural to rearrange or invent in order to bring about states of feeling that we like, just as a new tenant refurnishes a house.

The passions are a kind of thirst, inexorable and intense, for certain feelings or felt states. To find or invent "objects" (which are, more strictly speaking, relational structures) whose felt quality satisfies the passions—that for me is the activity of the artist, an activity which does not cease even to sleep.[19]

The intensity Motherwell describes is a two-way street: while it can be generated by the artist, from a Whiteheadian perspective it can also be catalyzed by artistic media. A couple of paragraphs later in this essay, Motherwell confirms art's relational properties when he notes, "color and space relations constitute such a means because from them can be made structures which exhibit the various patterns of reality."[20] "Patterns of reality" may well be shorthand for Whiteheadian constellations of energy, comprising not only actual entities but also more enduring forms, which only appear to be inert substances, even though, from a processist standpoint, they are just longer progressions with changes less clearly marked.

Not only is Motherwell's abstraction relational in the sense that actual occasions selectively prehend feelings in order to congregate available energy from already existent actual entities, but it also constitutes a mode of *emphasis*, another Whiteheadian concept crucially important for Motherwell. In the following statement, Whitehead joins these two qualities together with "aesthetic content," thus setting the stage for Motherwell's subsequent qualitative view of abstraction as a means for stressing some contents while obviating others in his art. In *Modes of Thought* Whitehead writes:

Mankind is distinguished from animal life by its emphasis on abstractions. The degeneracy of mankind is distinguished from its uprise by the dominance of chill abstractions, divorced from aesthetic content.[21]

In his 1970 lecture "The Universal Language of Children's Art and Modernism" for the "Conference on International Exchange in the Arts," Motherwell connected abstraction and emphasis in a statement that could be considered a description of Whitehead's actual entity and the prehensive aggressiveness giving rise to it. One might think of Motherwell's "complexity of particulars" in the following statement as actual entities, his "abstraction" as a prehensive process, and his view of emphasis as a lure catalyzing the consolidating forces making up an artwork:

Who does not love the complexity of particulars [actual entities] in reality? At the same time, one *must* abstract—that is, select from—in order to manage all reality at all. Meaning, after all, is a matter of emphasis, a selection; abstraction [part of any prehensive course of action] is the process of emphasis, no matter how relatively complex the work. To be a master of language is to be a master of emphasis.[22]

Emphasis in art involves not only directing one's attention to a given situation, a value, an idea, etc. but also making qualitative judgments about them. Motherwell signaled the significance of this tactic when he cited Mallarmé's imperative, *"to paint, not the thing, but the effect that it produces."*[23] Viewed in this manner, emphasis is prehensive sensing, abstraction is the overall activity of *concrescence* or the joining or growing together of forces on the basis of feeling, and the art object is the constellation of these self-generating forces that comprise an actual entity. In this way viewers are provided with opportunities to participate in the related process of turning artworks into yet other actual entities as they view and interpret them.

As Whitehead notes, "The growth of consciousness is the uprise of abstraction. It is the growth of emphasis."[24] In his paper for MoMA's 1951 symposium organized in conjunction with the exhibition "Abstract Painting and Sculpture in America," Motherwell rethinks this idea in terms of abstract art:

Abstraction is a process of emphasis, and emphasis vivifies life, as A.N. Whitehead said....

The need is for felt experience—intense, immediate, direct, subtle, unified, warm, vivid, rhythmic....Abstract art is an effort to close the void that modern men feel. Its abstraction is its emphasis.[25]

The reference to Whitehead's conceptualization of abstraction's emphasis as a means for enhancing life has to be understood in terms of the dynamic ways prehending energies give rise to the abstract concision of a momentary unitary form, i.e., the work of art per se. This resultant form might appear to be as enduring as the Egyptian pyramids, but even when these architectural wonders are viewed in terms of the eons comprising geologic ages or Darwinian evolution, their apparent long-term duration seems to be but a moment in time.

In 1951 Motherwell also provided special insight into his view of abstract art as a form of emphasis by referring to one of Whitehead's last essays "Mathematics and the Good." When asked to provide a summary of his overall work for the Library of Living Philosophers, Whitehead, who was then in ill health, instead submitted "Mathematics and the Good," a paper he had presented as a talk at Harvard the previous year, in addition to the requisite introductory autobiography. Rather than focusing on Whitehead's summary of approaches to mathematics, Motherwell preferred to think about "certain...asides..., for, in talking about mathematics as a way of thinking about pattern, he [Whitehead] points out that mathematics is thinking about certain patterns in concrete reality and ignoring others, and is consequently a form of abstraction—thought in this sense...is a form of emphasis. And so," Motherwell concludes "is art."[26]

While this summary correlates well with Whitehead's theory of prehension and demonstrates yet again the overall importance this process philosopher's theories had for Motherwell, a careful reading of his essay indicates an extraordinarily important idea that this artist may have so thoroughly assimilated that he did not deem it necessary to remark on it. This missing concept is the idea that abstraction can only be appreciated as truly profound if it draws on "some background of feeling...which is the awakening of infinitude to finite activity."[27] In his art Motherwell repeatedly finds ways to allude, if not to the infinites, at least to a far greater range of social, historical, and cultural background references that his titles in concert with his abstract forms are able to highlight. Pertinent examples include references to the death of the Mexican revolutionary Francisco "Pancho" Villa in the collage *Pancho Villa, Dead and Alive* (1943), either the Danish philosopher Søren Kierkegaard or Motherwell himself in *The Homely Protestant* (1948), Federico García Lorca's poem "Llanto por Ignacio Sánchez Mejías" mourning the death of this great Spanish bullfighter and for Motherwell the cessation of the Spanish Republic in his series of *Elegies to the Spanish Republic* (begun in the late 1940 and continued for decades), as well as the famous allegory Socrates narrated about the limits of empiricism *In Plato's Cave No. 1* (1972). Through his evocative titles Motherwell emphasizes certain narratives and in doing so surrounds his art with a penumbra of rich associations that imbue his abstract works with traces of potentially rich and varied meanings, thus providing in Whitehead's words "[a] value-experience, by the inflow from the infinite into the finite, deriving special character from the details and the totality of the finite pattern."[28]

Notes

1 Robert Motherwell, "'On the Humanism of Abstraction: The Artist Speaks" in Ashton and Banach, eds., *The Writings of Robert Motherwell*, p. 253.
2 Robert Motherwell, "'Expressionism." A two-page typescript (ca. 1950). Ashton and Banach, eds., *The Writings of Robert Motherwell*, p. 99.
3 Robert Motherwell, "'What Abstract Art Means to Me," *Museum of Modern Art Bulletin* 18, No. 3 (Spring, 1951): 12–13. Ashton and Banach, eds., *The Writings of Robert Motherwell*, p. 158.

4 Robert Motherwell, "'Robert Motherwell: A Conversation at Lunch'" (November 1962) in Terenzio, ed., *The Collected Writings of Robert Motherwell*, p. 139.
5 Robert Motherwell, "Letter from Robert Motherwell to Frank O'Hara, Dated August 18, 1965" in Terenzio, ed., *The Collected Writings of Robert Motherwell*, pp. 148 and 151.
6 Robert Motherwell, "The Modern Painter's World," *Dyn 1*, No. 6 (November, 1944): 9–14. Ashton and Banach, *The Writings of Robert Motherwell*, p. 27.
7 Whitehead, *Process and Reality*, p. 18.
8 Robert Motherwell, "Interview with Richard Wagener" (14 June 1974) in Terenzio, ed., *The Collected Writings of Robert Motherwell*, p. 215.
9 Robert Motherwell, "The New York School" (27 October 1950) in Terenzio, ed., *The Collected Writings of Robert Motherwell*, p. 78.
10 Robert Motherwell, "The New York School" (1950), Ashton and Banach, eds., *The Writings of Robert Motherwell*, p. 95.
11 Robert Motherwell, "Final Page of Letter to Unknown Party" (Early 1952) in Terenzio, ed., *The Collected Writings of Robert Motherwell*, p. 99. I would be remiss at this point not to mention D.W. Prall's *Aesthetic Analysis* in conjunction with the concept of relational structures. Whether Prall picked up this idea from Whitehead or developed it himself is a moot point, and yet in Prall's observation on page 34 of his *Aesthetic Analysis*, he refers not only to relations but also differences in patterns—two ideas crucial to Whitehead's metaphysics:

To show that one kind of relation is dependent on another all we need to do is exhibit variation in pattern constituted by this type of relation, while the pattern constituted by another type of relation must vary accordingly.

Mattison discovered a marginal note by Motherwell next to the following passage of Prall's text: "The perfect work of art then is one in which a term cannot be changed without affecting all the systems of relations." Mattison, *Robert Motherwell: The Formative Years*, p. 9.
12 Motherwell, "Notes on Mondrian and Chirico" (1942) in Ashton and Banach, eds., *The Writings of Robert Motherwell*, p. 15.
13 Robert Motherwell, "Preface to Duthuit's *The Fauvist Painters*" (1950) in Ashton and Banach, eds. *The Writings of Robert Motherwell*, p. 91.
14 Robert Motherwell, "Interview with Bryan Robertson, Addenda" (1965) in Terenzio, ed., *The Collected Writings of Robert Motherwell*, p. 142.
15 Whitehead, *Modes of Thought*, p. 167.
16 Whitehead, *Process and Reality*, 163.
17 Motherwell was well aware of Freud's early work in physiology with the scientist Ernst Wilhelm von Brücke at the University of Vienna. In his *Lectures on Physiology* (1874), von Brücke proposed the theory that living organisms are systems of energy. Freud extended this concept by applying it to the human personality. He looked at how the mind can transfer libidinous force, which he equated early in his professional career with all psychic energy, not just sexual force, and reflected on how this force can repress it and can sap it through fixations, resulting, in extreme cases, in neuroses and psychoses.
18 During the academic year of 1975–1976, when I lived in Motherwell's guesthouse in Greenwich, CT, while teaching at Yale University, we had many discussions about the relative merits of Freud and Jung. I contended that Jung was the greater aesthetician, while Motherwell championed Freud. To make his point, he gave

me a basic book on Freudian psychology because of its intelligent discussion of energy displacement. It appears that the first scholar to view Motherwell as Jungian rather than Freudian is Dore Ashton in *The New York School: A Cultural Reckoning*. She thinks the Jungian collective unconscious, with its related idea of individuals' reenacting enduring myths in their dreams, is more important for abstract expressionism than Freud's ideas, and she credits Motherwell as being responsible for disseminating this psychologist's ideas to his fellow artists. Dore Ashton, *The New York School: A Cultural Reckoning* (Middlesex: Penguin Books, 1979), pp. 124–125.

When referring to his series of *Elegies to the Spanish Republic*, Motherwell was always careful to qualify his assessment of these works conditionally as Jungian archetypes. The following statement by him is a characteristic example: "The *Elegies* use a basic pictorial language, in which I seem to have hit on an 'archetypal' image." Robert Motherwell, quoted in Jack D. Flam, "With Robert Motherwell" in *Robert Motherwell* (New York: Abbeville Press, 1983), p. 22.

19 Robert Motherwell, "Beyond the Aesthetic" (1946) in Ashton and Banach, eds., *The Writings of Robert Motherwell*, p. 54.

20 Robert Motherwell , "Beyond the Aesthetic" in Ashton and Banach, eds., *The Collected Writings of Robert Motherwell*, p. 55.

21 Whitehead, *Modes of Thought*, p. 123.

22 Robert Motherwell, "'The Universal Language of Children's Art, and Modernism," (1970) in Ashton and Banach, eds., *The Collected Writings of Robert Motherwell*, p. 270.

23 Motherwell, "Letter from Robert Motherwell to Frank O'Hara" in Terenzio, ed., *Collected Writings of Robert Motherwell*, p. 154.

24 Whitehead, *Modes of Thought*, p. 123.

25 Robert Motherwell, "'What Abstract Art Means to Me'" (1951) in Ashton and Banach, eds., *The Writings of Robert Motherwell*, p. 159.

26 Robert Motherwell, "The Rise and Continuity of Abstract Art," Lecture at Fogg Art Museum, Cambridge, Massachusetts (April 12, 1951). Dedalus Foundation Archives, IX.E, folder 1. N.B. only the final part of this lecture is published in Ashton and Banach, eds., *The Writings of Robert Motherwell*.

27 Alfred North Whitehead, "Mathematics and the Good" in Schilpp, ed., *The Philosophy of Alfred North Whitehead*, p. 679.

28 Whitehead, "Mathematics and the Good," p. 681.

4 Surrealism's Psychic Automatism, Motherwell's Plastic Automatism, and Whitehead's Process

The coming to the United States of the European surrealists, an often-told story, was important not only because it signified that New York was the new locus for international vanguard art during World War II, but also because it enabled American artists to become directly acquainted with recent works by some of the greatest figures in the history of modern art. Among the emigrants were the surrealists Breton, Salvador Dalí, Matta, Max Ernst, André Masson, Kurt Seligmann, and Yves Tanguy.[1] The points of contact between European painters and the group of artists who were to become abstract expressionists was not as many as one might presume. In addition to a language barrier (Breton and Masson among others did not speak English),[2] there was also a social one since many of the Europeans moved among New York's *haut monde* while most of the American painters were part of the Greenwich Village vanguard. With the exception of Arshile Gorky, Baziotes, and Motherwell, very few abstract expressionist painters were deeply involved with the Europeans.[3] The main influence of the temporary transplanting of the School of Paris to the United States was the realization by the Americans that the most creative art was now being made in their own country and that they could participate in it and might even contribute to modern art's development.

Because of his ability to understand French and his intellectual background, Motherwell became almost immediately involved with the surrealists. After teaching courses on modern art, contemporary architecture, and aesthetics during the winter of 1939 to 1940 at the University of Oregon, he decided not to resume studies in philosophy at Harvard, since Prall had died and Lovejoy had returned to Johns Hopkins; instead he planned to study archaeology and art history at Columbia on the advice of his former Harvard classmate, the aspiring composer Arthur Berger, whom he saw in Paris. Columbia professor Meyer Schapiro's article "Nature of Abstract Art," published in the first issue of *Marxist Quarterly* in January 1937, views abstractions as much more than mere design, and it was a significant reference for Motherwell. Decisive for attesting to crucial affiliations with the culture in which it was created, Schapiro's essay resonated with conversations in which Motherwell had participated at Harvard with Lovejoy and Whitehead, either personally or in terms of their published writings, that prepared him to view art as historically grounded in the cultures giving rise to them. During his first semester at Columbia, he often showed his paintings to Schapiro, who was one of his professors, and asked for his advice.[4] Realizing Motherwell's overriding interest in painting, Schapiro, according to Motherwell, encouraged him to become an artist rather than to pursue his art historical studies and suggested he meet some of the surrealists then living in New York. Motherwell recalled the situation in the following way:

> After some reflection, he [Schapiro] arranged that I study engraving with Kurt Seligmann. (Seligmann spoke English very well.) He was learned, and, as we would say nowadays, "square." Although I was interested in learning engraving, the thing was really a pretext (which we both understood) to help me to enter a bit into the French milieu. After all I couldn't just hang around.[5]

Many expatriate surrealists came to Seligmann's studio, and he would on several occasions take Motherwell on reciprocal visits. In this way, Motherwell met most members of this expatriate group and remained closely associated with them for several years. Although he enjoyed the stimulation of their company and participated in 1942 in "First Papers of Surrealism," an exhibition organized by Breton and Marcel Duchamp, Motherwell never became one of surrealism's adopted sons as did Matta and Gorky, even though he greatly appreciated its advanced view of creativity as involving one in an enlarged sense of self afforded by theories of the subconscious and unconscious.

Seligmann invited Motherwell and another student, Barbara Reis, the daughter of art collectors Rebecca and Bernard J. Reis, to accompany him and his wife on a trip to Mexico. At the last moment, the Seligmanns decided not to go because of financial complications abroad, and Matta and his wife were asked to take their place. Seligmann provided Motherwell with a letter of introduction to Wolfgang Robert Paalen, a German-Austrian painter and sculptor with a strong interest in philosophy and a member of the surrealist school, who had moved to Mexico in 1939.[6] Matta, then the youngest of the surrealists, became one of Motherwell's close friends. In the summer of 1941 the two painters, together with Matta's wife Patricia and Barbara Reis, went to Mexico. Speaking of the trip, Motherwell recalls it as an extensive course in surrealism:

> It was important in a special sense. In the three months of that summer of 1941, Matta gave me a ten-year education in Surrealism....Maria [Maria

Emilia Ferreira y Moyers, a Mexican playwright and actress whom Motherwell married] and I settled near Paalen till nearly Christmas time. Paalen was an intellectual, a man widely read; and it was with him that I got my postgraduate education in Surrealism, so to speak.[7]

Paalen dealt in Pre-Columbian art and became an eloquent spokesperson for American Indian culture. Combining his experience with modern, ancient, and traditional cultures, he regarded the artist in modern society as a self-chosen individual, who is responsible for describing what is significant in modern experience—a position Motherwell endorsed and perpetuated in his writings about art. However, according to Paalen, the modern artist, unlike creative individuals in the past, does not enjoy the benefits of a clearly defined subject matter:

> As long as art had a well defined and generally accepted function in the pattern of a coherent social life, the artist was provided with specific subject-matter—his only worry was over how to paint, not what to paint…the problem of how to paint can no longer be separated from the problem of what to paint. A given subject-matter today exists only for imitative tendencies, and for the mouthpieces of propaganda and advertising. But the problem of subject-matter has become crucial for all those who attempt to find in their art a general human significance.[8]

Paalen's question about what to paint was to have a substantial impact on Motherwell and the artists Baziotes, David Hare, Barnett Newman, and Rothko, who joined him in 1948 forming the short-lived school in New York City entitled Subjects of the Artists.

In 1944 when Motherwell participated in the prestigious symposium at Mount Holyoke College[9] and presented a paper later published as "The Modern Painter's World," his views paralleled Paalen's in terms of emphasizing painterly means rather than invoking mainly the unconscious as one's subject. Thus, he broke with Breton's orthodox surrealist view of psychic automatism as mainly a way to plumb the unconscious, which this French chief surrealist apologist regarded as a cognitive realm characterized by a strange iconography with which modern humanity had lost contact, i.e., becoming an "ideology,"[10] according to Motherwell, rather than a vital process for enriching one's subject matter, formal inventiveness, and responsiveness to one's chosen media. Motherwell explains:

> To give oneself over completely to the unconscious is to become a slave. But here it must be asserted at once that plastic automatism though perhaps not verbal automatism—as employed by modern masters, like Masson, Miró and Picasso, is actually very little a question of

the unconscious. It is much more a plastic weapon with which to invent new forms. As such it is one of the twentieth century's greatest formal inventions.[11]

Thinking about automatism as a collaboration between artist and his or her medium became a mainstay of Motherwell's attitude toward this technique. Although his approach has often been examined from a formalist perspective, it deserves to be understood from a Whiteheadian framework.

Paalen's theoretical views, but not his art, had such a tremendous impact on Motherwell that he arranged in 1945 for this artist and thinker's *Form and Sense* to be published as the first book in the Wittenborn series "Problems of Contemporary Art," which he was editing. The year 1941, when Motherwell had decided to remain in Mexico after his fellow travelers returned to New York in order to spend time with Paalen, was a critical time for this European expatriate as he was inaugurating the art magazine *Dyn,* based on the Greek word *Dynaton* meaning "the possible."[12] That same year Paalen also broke with the surrealists, so his thinking, while still based on surrealism's tenets, had diverged from Bretonian orthodoxy. To engage in extended conversations with Paalen, who took only certain aspects of surrealism while rejecting others, must have been illuminating and also liberating for Motherwell, who had previously only been acquainted with Seligmann's and his fellow surrealists' more traditional views as well as with Matta's quest to revitalize surrealism by returning to its roots. Paalen's studies of Pre-Columbian and Northwest Coast American Indian cultures no doubt had enabled Motherwell also to look at surrealism's generative principle, automatism, as a modern version of earlier cultures' time-honored methods for discovering personal truths, which had been interpreted in terms of myths and magic. In *Form and Sense*, Paalen distinguishes between automatism as divinely inspired truth and mere subjective interpretation:

The most complex art movement of the last fifteen years became particularly interested in an attempt to give a new collective basis to artistic creation through the liberation of the unconscious. This attempt led to the invention of various techniques belonging to a mode of expression that is called *automatism.*

The relevant aspects of automatism can be summarized as consisting of various kinds of techniques of *divination*, whose function is to sense unexpected images in aesthetically amorphous material. It is necessary to distinguish *subjective interpretation* from automatism. To interpret a given or to construct virtual images out of anecdotal representations cannot be called automatic invention. Certainly, to dream in an academic style is with equal certainty not an automatic activity. Salvador Dali has thus never made paintings which could be qualified as automatic.[13]

Paalen regards automatism as a means for beginning to plumb the wellsprings of truth; this technique, moreover, serves as crucially important source material for artistic expression, which then takes hold of this material and transforms it into artworks:

> For automatism, as well in painting as in poetry, can be no more than incantatory technique, and not creative expression. The verbal flow of the poet and the kaleidoscopic flow of the painter, emancipated in automatism, are nothing but raw material—and it is the great merit of surrealism to have taught us that it is this (and not the exterior world) that is the true raw material of the poet and the painter.[14]

Paalen's broad appreciation of earlier cultures and concomitant view of meaningful similarities between automatism and incantation had the net effect of discerning the generative principle of surrealist automatism to constitute one of the fundamental ways humankind has opened up vast internal and spiritual resources. As a committed modern artist, Paalen also respected the need to channel aspects of this vast repository into new and relevant modes of expression.

For Motherwell, Paalen's ideas must have been revelatory, because they permitted him to become a surrealist insofar as surrealism is the embodiment of an automatist process and to recognize the strengths as well as the limits of some of the surrealists' more representational artistic forms. When he returned to New York in November 1941, Motherwell ostensibly became a member of the surrealist group and even acted for a short time as one of the editors of its new periodical *VVV*. Because of his association with Paalen and *Dyn*, which was first published in April 1942, Yves Tanguy accused Motherwell in a *VVV* editorial meeting of being a traitor to this type of art, which he and some of his fellow surrealists regarded as far more than a mere artistic style and instead a fundamental outlook on life.[15]

In a letter of December 3, 1941 Motherwell invited noted American vanguard poet William Carlos Williams to become one of the magazine's editors and provided him with a summary definition of surrealism, including his own relation to it. In this letter he defines the movement in terms of the following four propositions:

> A short answer, as I understand the matter, would run like this: a. stimulation of the imagination—in the sense of enriching sensuous life by insisting on ignored aspects of reality, the invention of new objects of perception within reality, etc. b. the preservation of the dignity and value of personal feelings—a response to the felt need (in a world increasingly able to deal with physical nature, and potentially, with social relations) of

insisting that the only possible end of science and of a good society, the felt-content of the organism's experiencing, must not be annihilated or be held in contempt because it is not scientifically or sociologically useful. Hence the importance of the artist, etc. c. revolutionism—not so much in the sense of dwelling on the material difficulties and means (though this is implied), but revolution in the sense of increased consciousness, of consciousness of the possibilities inherent in experiencing. Emphasis therefore on novelty, invention, the disturbing, the strange— the power of feeling to move the organism. d. the dialectic—not so much in the Hegelian sense as constitution, the metaphysical nature of reality, or in the Marxist sense as the economic nature of society, but in the sense of a weapon for interpreting and synthesizing reality, as when Breton asks for a union between normal consciousness and the unconscious.[16]

All four of Motherwell's propositions are concerned with psychic automatism as a means for opening the creative mind to preconscious thoughts and unconscious drives. Although his approach is definitely influenced by his surrealist connections, it is also manifestly Whiteheadian, as indicated by such terms as "felt need," "felt-content," "emphasis," and "novelty," referring to prehensions and "organism." Because Motherwell considers this approach to be of great importance and full of unexplored possibilities, he thinks of himself for a time as a member of the surrealist clan as he explains in his letter:

> Through him [Meyer Schapiro] I came into contact with the surrealists —against whom I had many philosophical prejudices but they seemed to understand empirically the solution—or perhaps better, a solution to those problems of how to free the imagination in concrete terms, which are so baffling to an American. Until then, in short, I had been an observer, like a character in James; but with the advantage of having logical and plastic weapons with which to test my observations. Now I have taken a partisan stand, in the creative sense that the surrealism [sic] automatism is the basis of my painting, and in the theoretical sense that I find myself intellectually in accord with them. (The philosophical objections I once held against them no longer seem very relevant, nor a better epistemological statement of their position very important.)[17]

However, Motherwell's editorial connections with *VVV* proved to be short-lived and ended before the first issue was printed after he learned that Breton, Ernst, and Duchamp (who had also joined the staff) wanted him to raise money in addition to serving as one of the periodical's American editors.[18]

Once Motherwell learned of this fund-raising expectation, he promptly resigned from his position as editor.[19]

In the first surrealist manifesto of 1924, Breton defined surrealism's generative principle as "pure psychic automatism...the dictation of thought in the absence of all control exercised by reason and outside all moral or aesthetic concerns." French surrealist artist and writer Marcel Jean in *The History of Surrealist Painting* has elaborated on this term's meaning:

> the word is borrowed from psychiatry and designated involuntary, unconscious psychic-poetic happenings; but, as we have already seen, this word also contained the passion mixed with anguish of human beings in their relationship with machines that seem always to be on the point of liberating themselves from their creators and leading an autonomous existence.[20]

Psychic automatism was intended to be a means for opening pathways into the inner recesses of the mind and defying an overly mechanized world by excavating subterranean human depths. Members of this group hoped to find the true wellsprings of thought unhampered by the control of reason and a priori aesthetic or moral attitudes—in other words, to release humans from the bondage of consciousness and thus enable them to create a new reality.

Factually, surrealism means simply "super-realism," a definition antithetic to abstract and predominately formalist art. Some surrealist painters like Dalí, Ernst, and René Magritte took surrealism to be a form of hyper-realism. They employed automatism as an initial type of free-association, enabling them to devise arresting and strange combinations of realistic elements in an effort to illustrate dreams and fantasies. Max Ernst's title for his "Documents of Modern Art Series" book *Beyond Painting* indicates that his art had moved to a strange incantatory realm. His work consequently pictures a personal cosmology intended to enrich the content of modern art with evocative subjects that join past and present imagery as well as fine art, nineteenth-century popular culture, and scientific illustrations. Art historian Robert Goldwater in *Primitivism in Modern Art* has either fairly or unfairly criticized this type of surrealism for being illustrative. Because artists of this persuasion attempt to make such conscious highly evocative images as fantasies and daydreams that need to remain on the periphery of consciousness if they are to be appreciated as truly strange, evocative, and chimerical, Goldwater suggests they are impoverishing surrealism by forcing a more literal reading antithetic to the "level, at which 'real' and 'unreal' fuse and lose their [separate] meaning." [21]

In 1940s New York, the supra-real brand of surrealism never gained a wide following among the formative abstract expressionists, who were convinced by the examples of postimpressionism, German expressionism, and French cubism, among other abstract modern styles, to respect the surface of the canvas and create a relatively flat space rather than relying on such illusionist means as quattrocentro Italian painting techniques as had Dalí. For Goldwater, following such surrealists as Dalí and Ernst would represent an unfortunate retreat to traditional painting. And yet, despite the reservations of such a leading figure as Goldwater, among others, Motherwell in the early 1940s was able to embrace Ernst's figurative work and even convinced him not to destroy the plaster casts for his sculptures as he intended to do.[22] At the time, one of the foremost mid-twentieth-century American critics Clement Greenberg was so repulsed by what he considered to be surrealism's deception that he made the tenets of cubism the guiding principle of his often prescriptive criticism, which was purgative in its steadfast reliance on the assumed essential and inherent qualities of painting, which for him was most importantly the inviolable surface of the canvas.[23]

Despite Greenberg's orientation, many emerging abstract expressionists in the late 1940s continued to prize abstract surrealist art as a point of departure. Instead of picturing their dreams as equivalents of the so-called real world, most abstract expressionists populated their paintings with beings of a new abstract order arising from confrontations with their chosen media. Some of them proclaimed their automatism to have its origins in their engagements with this media as well as their own unconscious, and this approach, as we will see, validated Motherwell term plastic automatism. Moreover, many of these artists considered automatism to be largely determined by painters working intuitively with a given medium's advantages and drawbacks, rather than constituting an initial free association subsequently rendered in a painstaking manner according to traditional academic standards.

During the early 1940s Motherwell made occasional entries in an informal journal. On August 3, 1942 he referred to a statement that Mondrian made to Ernst, when both were living in New York: "You and I are the only true surrealists," Mondrian pointed out, "we see the same reality. The only thing that is different is the surface appearance of our pictures." Motherwell annotated the statement with the following remark: "The element of truth in the remark is so isolated from other truth, it has the appearance of a *bon mot*."[24] Mondrian's observation made a lasting impression on Motherwell, perhaps, because it explains the direction in which his art was moving during this period. Already in 1942 he was combining aspects of modern geometric abstraction and surrealism in his work and was uniting them under a modern-art rubric that is a coupling of cubist rationality and a generalized understanding of surrealism, as a type of automatism. Motherwell later described abstract expressionism as a blending of these two attitudes:

So that historically, though it has very little visual resemblance to either, "abstract expressionism" is in part, I think, a fusion of certain Surrealist means, above all plastic "automatism", with the Cubists' insistence that the picture speak as a picture in strictly pictorial language. I would say that our painting tends to be metaphysical.[25]

In addition, Motherwell has characterized his own artistic struggle in terms of forging a dialectic between automatic and formal means as well as organic and geometric approaches to beauty. Expressionism, then, is not one of the parents of its namesake abstract expressionism—psychic or plastic automatism is.[26] However, rather than blindly accepting surrealism and automatism as givens, Motherwell regards them as tactics available for use and transformation—methods replete with possibilities.

Motherwell's friendship with Ernst, who had been a noted Cologne Dadaist before becoming a surrealist, encouraged him to search for surrealism's sources in dada, an investigation that led in 1951 to the publication of his magisterial anthology *The Dada Painters and Poets*. "It was part of an effort to teach myself Surrealism systematically," he explained. "It was obvious that Dada was the older brother of Surrealism, and my original intention was to make a second volume on Surrealism."[27] He viewed dada as an important precursor to surrealism and suggested in his Introduction to *The Dada Painters and Poets* that surrealism was essentially Breton's transformation of dada."[28] When his anthology was published in 1951 after seven years of research, it had little, if any, influence on the abstract expressionists who had already reached their artistic maturity and achieved signatures styles, even though it did have a tremendous impact on the next generation of artists, some of whom became known as neo-dadaists, such as Jasper Johns, Allan Kaprow, and Motherwell's former student at Black Mountain College, Robert Rauschenberg.

Among the surrealists' most favored poets and preferred sources of inspiration was French symbolist Arthur Rimbaud, who wrote, "Our pale reason hides the infinite from us."[29] This insight sums up an attitude that a number of artists and poets have endorsed since the romantic era in the late eighteenth and early nineteenth centuries. They realized that the mind, failing to express the feelings of the heart, often acts as a prison for the spirit by tying it to established forms of rationality. To escape these encumbering ideologies and embrace the unknown, it was necessary to break with the constraints of consciousness in order to find other modes of expression. Rimbaud's solution implies mystical affiliations, even though he credits himself with these powers rather than attributing them to a transcendent being. According to Geneva School literary critic Marcel Raymond in his classic study *From Baudelaire to Surrealism*:

Rimbaud, the demonical thaumaturge, abandons himself only to recover himself, to enjoy his will to power and attempt to capture supernatural forces for his own profit. He is a sorcerer rather than a mystic, and it is only intermittently that he can forget his transcendent egoism.[30]

Rimbaud remains the hero of his own work even when he "cultivates his soul," goes beyond the rational in order to embrace a heightened internal spirituality, and creates a language that is as much a revelation to himself as to anyone else. His work comprises a type of psychic automatism capable of freeing himself of reason and allowing himself the opportunities to create intuitively and spontaneously by taking his work on the faith that it will mean something. He follows Charles Baudelaire, one of Motherwell's long-term favorites, particularly for his unapologetic embrace of the modern world, who observed, "Next to the pleasure of being surprised, there is no greater pleasure than to cause surprise."[31] Thus, for creative individuals working to release themselves from habitual ways of looking at the world, art's most pleasurable aspect is its capacity to amaze, confound, and entrance. Artists of this persuasion took their actions on faith, in the belief that they were capable of portending momentous significance, so that they refrained from censoring their emerging creations when working in order to provide themselves with opportunities for creating without the shackles of their own socially and historically conditioned judgment.

The surrealists became expert colonizers of the history of art and literature as they searched for prototypes and fellow kinsman, including such painters as Hieronymus Bosch and Arcimboldo as well as such objects as tribal masks, antiques, and curios capable of conjuring a sense of wonder. With free associational techniques of psychic automatism and the parlor game called the Exquisite Corpse, surrealists armed themselves with images of the miraculous as they updated improvisatory ways of making art. In addition to Rimbaud, one of their early revered forerunners was the then little-known nineteenth-century French poet Isidore-Lucien Ducasse, who chose the pseudonym Comte de Lautréamont and courted the marvelous—a key surrealist term—in his captivating descriptions in Les *Chants de Maldoror* (1869), among them his notably poetic vision of a young boy as "beautiful as the chance meeting on a dissecting-table of a sewing-machine and an umbrella." Because automatism is a method for courting the irrational and escaping the confines of established reason, this inspired approach has an even longer history reaching back to German and French progenitors of romanticism and even earlier to tribal shamans. Viewed in terms of a longer historical trajectory, surrealism and its incantatory technique psychic automatism can be regarded as an updating of the ways humans open themselves to fascinating and mysterious aspects of the world even as they defy the limits of straightforward rationality.

For visual artists, automatism can begin with the freeform, absent-minded activity of scribbling, which Motherwell calls doodling:

> But you have to think of doodling in Abstract Expressionism as on the scale of Michelangelo would have doodled, or Rubens....I think doodling is one of the alternative ways of drawing. Paul Klee, after his maturity, invariably begins with doodling.
>
> I know that all the classic Tanguys began as doodles....Many Max Ernsts did. All Miró's do. All Arps do. According to his son, Jean Renoir began his picture with color-spot doodles, and then turned them into girls, still-lifes or landscapes.[32]

Motherwell views this process as a revelatory way for artists to begin working by seriously mining their own purposefully non-directed activity. In doing so, they avail themselves of opportunities to avoid inhibitions and discover aspects of their innermost selves before moving to the aesthetic level of working with the new possibilities such a procedure afforded them.[33] Regarding doodling as a means for plumbing the unconscious or at least capturing aspects of the preconscious before it has been disciplined by social and cultural constraints, Motherwell attests that automatism can be of great formal value to abstract painters:

> To put it another way, if one is interested in abstract art, and starts a priori to make an abstraction, the human mind seems to be monotonous and limited: one makes squares or circles or crosses or triangles. Basic, rudimentary geometric forms. Now supposing you wanted to make an abstract picture, that's to say, you wanted a picture that didn't carry normal representation in it, but at the same time, you wanted an abstract picture as rich as nature. The only known means of doing it is through the various modes of automatism.[34]

Automatism, then, is a method in which artists encourage their minds to wander aimlessly in the first stages of creation and refrain from inhibiting thoughts about how the finished work will look. Eschewing calculation, artists open themselves to intuitive and creative play.

In 1959, in his review article of MoMA's retrospective of Spanish surrealist Juan Miró's art,[35] Motherwell revived the term "plastic automatism," which he had initially employed in 1944 in "The Modern Painter's World" to refer to European surrealists, even though, as indicated, he already had moved from Breton's orthodoxy to a more innovative approach predicated on collaborations with the artist's chosen media. In his piece on Miró, Motherwell describes plastic automatism as a means to replace surrealism's psychic automatism and also a way to signal his substantial rethinking of this improvisatory process, which he viewed as being of the utmost significance.[36] In fact, Motherwell regarded plastic automatism as crucially important for the development of abstract expressionism's genesis:

> Nevertheless, my conviction is that, more than any other single thing, the introduction and acceptance of the theory of automatism brought about a different look into our painting. We worked more directly and violently, and ultimately on a much larger scale physically than the surrealists ever had. It [plastic automatism] was the germ, historically, of what later came to be called abstract expressionism.[37]

Because Motherwell considered this creative approach to be the single most significant factor in abstract expressionism's development, it will help to look at how he understood this technique, while considering the crucial role Whitehead's processist theory played in his rethinking of it.

For the aforementioned conference on "The Creative Use of the Unconscious by the Artist and by the Psychotherapist," Motherwell summarized how he employed automatism:

> I usually begin a picture with a "doodle," or with a liquid puddle like a Rorschach image (but not pressed together), or with a line and a dot, or a piece of paper dropped at random on what will be a collage. Then the struggle begins, and endures throughout the state of anxiety that is ineffable, but obliquely recorded in the inner tensions of the finished canvas. The struggle has inexorable moral values—no nostalgia, no sentimentalism, no propaganda, no discourse, no autobiography, no violation of the canvas as a surface (since it *is* one), no clichés, no predetermined endings, no seduction, no charm, no relaxation, no mere taste, no obviousness, no coldness; or, oppositely, for me, it must have immediacy, passion or tenderness, *beingness*, as such, detachment, sheer presence as a modulation of the flat picture plane, true invention and search, light, an unexpected end, mainly warm colors, and black and white, a certain stalwartness.[38]

In addition to regarding this process in terms of the positive and negative conditions of what to include in his work and also what to exclude from it, which Motherwell equates with "moral values," he implies that this process is tripartite, with a beginning, middle, and final stage. As a three-part method, this process approximates the steps involved in Whitehead's processist theory, in particular the first stage of identifying which prehended energies will be selected, the second one of bringing together this prehended material, followed by the final process of creating a new actual occasion, notable for its novelty. In fact, Whitehead's description in *Process and Reality* of the three different stages involved in the origination of an actual entity, which I have been equating with the creation of an artwork, parallels Motherwell's steps so closely as to serve as a model and possible source for them. "The analysis of the formal constitution of an actual entity," Whitehead details in this book, "has given three stages in the process of feeling: (i) the responsive phase, (ii) the supplemental stage, and (iii) the satisfaction."[39] We can equate the first responsive phase, which Whitehead terms "pure reception of the actual world in its guise of objective datum for aesthetic synthesis"[40] with Motherwell's doodling—the need to have something with which to begin—an antecedent potentiality so to speak. Whitehead refers to the second stage as being "governed by the private ideal, gradually shaped in the process itself; whereby the many feelings, derivatively felt as alien, are transformed into a unity of aesthetic appreciation immediately felt as private." This prehensive phase, described as "assum[ing] an emotional character" and constituting "the aesthetic supplement" whereby "there is an emotional appreciation of the contrasts and rhythms inherent in the unification of the objective content in the concrescence of one actual occasion" (an actual entity) is akin to Motherwell's second stage whereby the artist puzzles over his or her initial marks to see what implicit structures they might portend and how he or she might cohere them into a work of art. The final part of this triadic breakdown of creativity into a "vector situation" is the culmination Whitehead calls "satisfaction," and Motherwell deems the work of art per se. Apropos this parallel, Whitehead characterizes in *Modes of Thought* this type of satisfaction in terms of the feeling an actual entity experiences as "absolute, individual self-enjoyment."[41]

It is highly doubtful Motherwell ever consciously identified or articulated the parallels between plastic automatism and Whitehead's process metaphysics I have briefly outlined; most likely Whitehead's system became such an important foundational model for Motherwell's thinking about creativity that it unconsciously served him a few years later when he first met the European surrealist expatriates in New York as a criterion for critiquing and rethinking their theory of psychic automatism. An example of Whitehead's concept of consciousness's viability as opposed to the shadowy realm surrounding it, which provides a foundation for Motherwell's transformation of surrealist psychic automatism, is this thinker's view of consciousness as a quivering force. Writing poetically in *Process and Reality*, Whitehead evokes consciousness in the following manner. "[E]ven at its brightest," he says, "there is a small focal region of clear illumination, and a large penumbral region of experience which tells of intense experience in dim apprehension," before adding, "The simplicity of clear consciousness is no measure of the complicity of complete experience." In this same passage he also emphasizes that "this character of our experience suggests that consciousness is the crown of experience, only occasionally attained, not its necessary base."[42] Whitehead's observation thus enables us to analogize the process of prehending forces culminating in concrescences in terms of dimly seen patterns (gestalts) that slowly come into focus, i.e., works of art.[43]

In the first paper in which Motherwell notably rethinks psychic automatism, which was first written, as noted earlier, for "Arts Plastique" and was appropriately renamed plastic automatism, he forges a synthesis between surrealist and nonobjective approaches to painting. He does so by shifting responsibility from the artist as strategic originator of a work of art to a more democratic conversation between painter and medium—a tactic entirely consistent with Whitehead's process theory in which creation results from self-generating forces rather than that from the solitary outside agential roles artists have traditionally assumed. This shift necessitates upholding such a material as paint as the ideal medium for directly responding to an artist's innermost thoughts while also documenting them:

> In the greatest painting, the painter communes with himself. Painting is his thought's medium. Others are able to participate in this communion to the degree they are spiritual. But for the painter to communicate with all, *in their own terms*, is for him to take on their character, not his own.
> Painting is a medium in which the mind can actualize itself; it is a medium of thought. Thus painting, like music, tends to become its own content.[44]

Although plastic automatism is not directly referenced in this passage, it is implied, as is the idea that Freudian preconscious thoughts can be regarded as participating in nonverbal conversations with the artist's chosen media, making them irresistible means for transposing preconscious and prehensive contents into forms works of art can accept.

Motherwell's most extensive discussion of this improvisational technique as a means for opening oneself to creativity is his essay on Miró. Occasioned by Miró's second MoMA retrospective in the spring of 1959, Motherwell's piece was published in the May issue of *Art News* before this show closed, thus ensuring it undeniable relevancy and a wide readership. Pertinent to this part of our discussion on Motherwell, Whitehead, and plastic automatism is the fact that this artist characterizes this incantatory technique strictly in terms of Freud's preconscious in which intuitive realizations—prehensive vectors of energy, using Whitehead's terminology for noncognitive apprehension—are not repressed and therefore can readily be summoned with a little conscious effort. In this piece Motherwell explains, "The Unconscious is inaccessible to the will by definition; that which is reached is the fluid and free 'fringes of the mind' called the 'preconscious,' and consciousness constantly intervenes in the process." He begins his analysis of plastic automatism by describing how Miró employs a free-associative technique to seed his previously prepared painterly ground with intuitions, which are more preconscious than unconscious. These intuitions can also be considered prehensive in the sense that this type of spontaneously self-generative feeling—equivalent to quantum mechanics' inherent randomness—comes before the creation of a new entity and thus the apprehension of it. Then, in order to become involved with these preconscious or prehensive energies, one must refrain, according to Motherwell, from "'moral or aesthetic a priori prejudices' (to cite André Breton's official definition of surrealism), for obvious reasons for anyone who wants to dive into the depths of being."[45] From a Whiteheadian perspective, there is not one agent governing the spontaneous collection of prehensive forces, since this philosopher aims to move beyond the legacy of substances as inert materials subject to overweening agents by theorizing a fecund world of electromagnetic fields of energies at work. Plastic automatism's get-acquainted period thus occurs between the artist's and his or her chosen material, during the process of doodling.

Motherwell concludes this first part of his analysis of automatism by citing curator James Johnson Sweeney's interview with Miró some years earlier when the Spanish artist revealed:

> What is most interesting to me today is the material I am working with. It supplies the shock which suggests the form just as the cracks in the wall suggested shapes to Leonardo. For this reason I always work on several canvases at once. I start a canvas without a thought of what it may become. I put it aside after the first fire has abated. I may not look at it again for months. Then I take it out and work at it coldly like an artisan, guided strictly by rules of composition after the first shock of suggestion has cooled ... first the suggestion, usually from the material: second, the conscious organization of these forms; and third the compositional enrichment.[46]

From Miró's explanation of his working process, we can conclude that plastic automatism provided the abstract expressionists with a type of creative summons. In Whiteheadian terms it is a question of spontaneously "feeling" the possibilities in order to draw together those capable of comprising a new occasion. The resultant actual entity making up this highly conceptual yet improvisational type of art is predicated on the congregating forces that comprise the art object per se.

Part of plastic automatism's attraction in the 1940s when psychology was referred to in films, books, and even discussed daily by New York cab drivers[47] can be found in the permission it grants artists to transfer the initial responsibility for creating a work of art to their preconscious, the partially accessible unconscious other residing within them. This other, however, is called forth via artists' engagements with their chosen media. In its initial stage, then, plastic automatism cultivates aspects of the unknown—traditionally personified as the artist's muse—which was assumed to dwell within humans as an eminently creative potential. The putative traces of this purported preconscious then become the incentive for the known self's or the ego's investigations of its media and conversely the media's examination of this ego. This dialectical process culminates in a self-created work of art, an actual entity; in abstract expressionism it has been equated with a particular artist's enlarged sense of self.

Lest one think that plastic automatism could become a rote method, it helps to remember Motherwell's revealing and humbling admission in 1965 to New York critic Max Kozloff:

> My pictures…would disclose crimes—layers of consciousness, of willing. They are a succession of humiliations resulting from the realization that only in a state of quickened subjectivity—of freedom from conscious notions, and with what I always suppose to be secondary or accidental colors and shapes—do I find the unknown, which nevertheless I recognize when I come upon it, for which I am always searching.[48]

Notes

1 Many other artists-in-exile came to the United States during those years: Josef Albers, Marcel Breuer, Lyonel Feininger (an American expatriate, who was born in New York City and lived for several decades in Germany), Naum Gabo, Walter Gropius, Fernand Léger, Piet Mondrian, László Moholy-Nagy, Amédée Ozenfant, and Mies van der Rohe.

2 Robert Motherwell, Letter to Michael Weaver, 22 April 1966. My notes pertaining to this letter were made in 1975 when it was in Motherwell's possession in Greenwich, CT. Since that time, its whereabouts are unknown.

3 John Jones, Interview with Robert Motherwell, 173 East 94th Street, NYC. 25 October 1965. The present location of this interview is unknown as is the letter to Weaver referenced in footnote number 2.

4 Motherwell's apartment when he moved to Manhattan and started taking classes at Columbia was on West 11th Street near Schapiro's residence.

5   Motherwell, "Interview with Sidney Simon: 'Concerning the Beginnings of the New York School: 1939–1943'" in Robert Motherwell, "On Not Becoming an Academic" in Terenzio, ed., *The Collected Writings of Robert Motherwell*, p. 157.

6   Martica Sawin, email to author, 15 November 2018. Although Motherwell has recounted that Matta introduced him to Paalen, Sawin in the course of researching material for *Surrealism in Exile and the Beginning of the New York School* (Cambridge: MIT Press, 1995) found documentation supporting Seligmann's role in providing Motherwell with a letter of introduction to Paalen.

7   Motherwell, "Interview with Sidney Simon: 'Concerning the Beginnings of the New York School: 1939–1943'" in Robert Motherwell, "On Not Becoming an Academic" in Terenzio, ed., *The Collected Writings of Robert Motherwell*, p. 159.

8   Wolfgang Paalen, "Introduction," *Form and Sense: Problems in Contemporary Art* (New York: Wittenborn and Co., 1945), n.p.

9   According to Glifford, the topic of the symposium was "The Crisis and Our Crisis." Among the attendants were such luminaries as Hannah Arendt and Claude-Lévi Strauss. Clifford, "Chronology" in Flam, Rogers, and Clifford, eds., *Robert Motherwell Paintings and Collages: A Catalogue Raisonné, 1941–1991* Volume 6, p. 188.

10 The persistence of this surrealist view is evident in the letter written by the formative abstract expressionists Adolph Gottlieb and Mark Rothko to the *New York Times* when they state, "To us art is an adventure into an unknown world, which can be explored only by those willing to take risks." For this observation about this well-known letter, I am gratefully indebted to Danto's essay "The 'Original Creative Principle': Motherwell and Psychic Automatism" in Rosand, ed., *Robert Motherwell on Paper: Drawings, Prints, Collages*, p. 43.

    Motherwell uses the word ideology to refer to the surrealists' endorsement of an established or anticipated albeit strange and haunting iconography. Diamonstein, "An Interview with Robert Motherwell" in Arnason, *Robert Motherwell*, p. 228.

11 Robert Motherwell, "The Modern Painter's World" in Ashton and Banach, eds., *The Writings of Robert Motherwell*, p. 34.

12 It is perhaps no coincidence that in 1947 Motherwell was one of the originating editors for the new periodical *Possibilities*. Given his history with Paalen and *Dyn*, he may have suggested the title.

13 Paalen, *Form and Sense*, p. 34.

14 Paalen, *Form and Sense*, p. 34.

15 Robert Motherwell, Conversation with author, Greenwich, CT (19 October 1974).

16 Robert Motherwell, Letter to William Carlos Williams, 3 December 1941 in Terenzio, ed., *The Collected Writings of Robert Motherwell*, pp. 17–18.

17 Robert Motherwell, Letter to William Carlos Williams, 3 December 1941 in Terenzio, , ed., *The Collected Writings of Robert Motherwell*, p. 17.

18 Motherwell, Letter to Michael Weaver, 22 April 1966.

19 Motherwell was replaced by the eminent American playwright, essayist, and theater critic Lionel Abel, who also vacated the position before the first issue was published. David Hare, who became the third American to join the staff, served as the journal's editor throughout its three published issues.

20 Marcel Jean and Arpad Mezei, *The History of Surrealist Painting*, trans. Simon Watson Taylor (New York: Grove Press, 1967), p. 118.

21 Robert Goldwater, *Primitivism in Modern Art* (Rev. ed., New York: Vintage Books, 1967), pp. 220–221.

22 Years later, in appreciation for saving these sculptures from destruction, Ernst bestowed on Motherwell one of the bronze casts of *The King Playing with the Queen* (1944), which Motherwell proudly exhibited in his Greenwich, CT, home.

23 Clement Greenberg, "Toward a New Laocoon," *Partisan Review*, 7 (July–Aug. 1940), pp. 296–310. Greenberg defines the limits of painting in this early article.

24 Robert Motherwell, Unpublished Notes, 3 Aug. 1942. According to these notes, Max Ernst in turn repeated this statement to Motherwell.

25 David Sylvester, "Painting as Existence," Interview with Robert Motherwell. [conducted by David Sylvester as Painting as Self-Discovery. London: BBC, 22 Oct. 1960.] TS, Dedalas Foundation Archives.

26 Both of Motherwell's opinions restated in the above two statements have their source in Bryan Robertson, "Art, N.Y.," Interview with Robert Motherwell (New York: Channel 13, 15 December 1964), TS. Dedalus Foundation.

27 Max Kozloff, "An Interview with Robert Motherwell: How I admire my colleagues," *Artforum* 4, No. 1 (September, 1965): 37.

28 Robert Motherwell, ed., "Introduction," *The Dada Painters and Poets: An Anthology*, Documents of Modern Art XI (1951; rpt. New York: George Wittenborn, Inc., 1967), p. xxvi.

29 Marcel Raymond, *From Baudelaire to Surrealism*, Documents of Modern Art, Volume 10 (New York: Wittenborn, Schultz, 1950), p. 32

30 Raymond, *From Baudelaire to Surrealism*, p. 32.

31 Raymond, *From Baudelaire to Surrealism*, p. 214.

32 Kozloff, "An Interview with Robert Motherwell," p. 34. The source for Motherwell's continued use of the word doodling appears to be Frank Capra's 1936 film *Mr. Deeds Goes to Town* in which the namesake character, played by Cary Cooper, defends himself in a courtroom by pointing to the character Emile von Haller, a Viennese expert, billed as "the most eminent psychiatrist in the world," [a playful jab at Freud], who is characterized as "doodling"—idly sketching—while listening to others' testimonies. This film's usage of the term soon became widespread; it was internationally ratified the following year, according to the OED, when *The Manchester Guardian* described, "Doodling ... [as] fidgeting about pictorially with a pen or pencil at odd moments to pass the time... .," and noted, "In Australia... [caterers] have provided special menu cards with plenty of space on them in the hope of luring doodlers into doodling on these instead of on the table cloth."

33 Diamonstein, "An Interview with Robert Motherwell" in Arnason, ed., *Robert Motherwell*, p. 228.

34 Kozloff, "An Interview with Robert Motherwell," p. 34.

35 Robert Motherwell, "The Significance of Miró," *Art News* 58, No. 4 (May 1959): 32–33, 65–67. The longer version of this essay is found in Ashton and Banach, eds., *The Writings of Robert Motherwell*, pp. 188–193.

36 Some of the ideas explored in this chapter build on my previous work differentiating the abstract expressionists' approach to automatism from that of the surrealists. Robert Hobbs, "Surrealism and Abstract Expressionism: From Psychic to Plastic Automatism" in Isabelle Dervaux, *Surrealism USA* (New York: National Academy Museum in conjunction with Hatje Cantz Publishers, 2005).

37   Robert Motherwell, "Interview with Sidney Simon: 'Concerning the Beginnings of the New York School: 1939–1943'" in Terenzio, ed., *The Collected Writings of Robert Motherwell*, p. 163.
38   Robert Motherwell, "A Process of Painting," (5 October 1963) in Terenzio, ed., *The Collected Writings of Robert Motherwell*, pp. 140–141.
39   Whitehead, *Process and Reality*, p. 212.
40   Both this and other references to Whitehead's three stages found in this paragraph come from *Process and Reality*, p. 212.
41   Whitehead, *Modes of Thought*, p. 151.
42   Whitehead, *Process and Reality*, p. 267.
43   Adrienne Dengerink Chaplin, *The Philosophy of Susanne Langer: Embodied Meaning in Logic, Art and Feeling* (London, New York, and Oxford: Bloomsbury Academic, 2020), pp. 116–117.
44   Robert Motherwell, "The Modern Painter's World" in Ashton and Banach, eds., *The Writings of Robert Motherwell*, p. 32.
45   Robert Motherwell, "The Significance of Miró" in Ashton and Banach, eds., *The Collected Writings of Robert Motherwell*, p. 192.
46   Robert Motherwell, "The Significance of Miró" in Ashton and Banach, eds., *The Writings of Robert Motherwell*, pp. 192–193. Notably Miró and Whitehead independently devise tripartite structures for creativity. When he discusses Miró's approach, Motherwell puts a decidedly Whiteheadian spin on it.
47   In the 1970s one of Motherwell's favored analogies was to say that psychology was so prevalent that it was even a topic of conversation with cab drivers.
48   Kozloff, "An Interview with Robert Motherwell: 'How I admire my colleagues,'" *Artforum* 4, No. 1 (September 1965): p. 34.

5   Motherwell's Collage Aesthetic

Whitehead's process metaphysics provided Motherwell with an interconnected rationale enabling him to understand the overall dynamics of both organic and inorganic realms in terms of never-ending creative pulsations of energy (called "feelings"). These felt velocities result in ongoing formations of actual entities, which in turn serve as sources for yet other actual entities taking the form of viewer's responses and thus other subsequent works of art. Whitehead's system encouraged Motherwell to theorize a meaningful type of abstract art first in terms of sets of related patterns of energies before thinking about how such abstractions can offer a preeminent means of emphasis, since a personalized form of abstraction, according to this philosopher, determines its own criteria for inclusion and exclusion. Because of his grounding in Whitehead's progressions, Motherwell was able to reconfigure, as I have suggested, the surrealist improvisatory technique of psychic automatism as "plastic automatism," based on the model of Freud's preconscious and this psychoanalyst's concomitant view of human drives and instincts as displacements of energy.

In order to appreciate how Motherwell redirects in his art Whitehead's process metaphysics, based on a grasp of the randomness of the universe on an atomic level, I will analyze some of his early collages as relational systems (i.e., patterns of energies), as well as distinct means of emphases (or becoming), depending first on the artist's participation in the work's creation and then on percipients' responses, constituting a second process, resulting in a layering of two different overlapping sets of actual entities. In this situation, there are two different approaches to a given collage, encompassing the registers of first—using Whitehead's terminology—concrescing (that is cohering) prehended (noncognitive and spontaneous apprehensive) energies forming the patterns comprising the collage itself, and second, the many actual occasions activated through individual viewers' connections with the coalescing energies in this same collage. Instead of looking at Motherwell's collages, as Sherburne recommends of all art, as only lures for feeling, as they most certainly are in the second stage, I am theorizing the works as first incarnating in themselves different types of feelings or energies, including the artist's, which are often held in place through interlocking tensions, to create the event that is the art object. Considered in this way Motherwell's collages, especially his early ones, can be understood as active works that appear to be caught in the process of concrescing prehended forces, so that viewers are encouraged to enter into the game of completing individual pieces as interpreted actual occasions. This second-order concrescence helps to explain how the apparent lack of finish found in a number of abstract expressionist works, including Motherwell's collages and paintings, functions when analyzed from a Whiteheadian perspective. I am suggesting that we need to think of Motherwell's art in these two ways in order to comprehend how it operates. We might conclude that some of his artworks, particularly his collages from the early 1940s, are purposefully engaged in open-ended types of becoming—that is, as prehended feelings or energies appearing *in media res*, thereby inducing viewers to work in tandem with the concrescing energies of the art before them. In this way, each collage becomes a catalyst, giving rise to multiple works: again, the first piece is the artist's collaboration with his or her media, the art object per se, and the second is the interpreted work that is recreated by each discerning viewer entering into a conversation with a given collage's prehended feelings.[1]

In undertaking this Whiteheadian reading of Motherwell's collages, it is imperative to go beyond the artist's articulated intentions pertaining to the specific emotions he was experiencing at the time a given piece was created, particularly in light of the already examined distinctions Motherwell makes between emotion and feeling. We need also to embrace Whitehead's imperative to move, at all costs, beyond a Cartesian emphasis on humans (artists) as the preeminent form givers by viewing creativity as a collaborative coming together of different congregating forces. The reason for this move from a biographic interpretation, which would certainly be legitimate and relevant in a number of other circumstances, is to see how an entire range of motivations (feelings/energies), including those of the artist but certainly not limited to this individual, coalesce in unique works of art into newly prehended constellations. These ensuing concrescences take from the velocities giving rise to them, resulting in more enduring patterns of forces, constituting in each instance the actual entity and the collage itself. For this reason, we need to be wary of accepting Motherwell's account of *The Tearingness of Collaging* (1957) as only being concerned with its genesis "during some of the most tormented and exhausted years of my life, [making] the tearing... equivalent to murdering symbolically"[2] as the only definitive reading for this work. If we were to accept this interpretation, Motherwell's passionate response would constitute an emotional overlay that interrupts and subsumes under its auspices the individual felt qualities of each of the participating materials—including their individual semiotic references. In addition to moving beyond Motherwell's statements of intent or his own assessments of the meanings of his collages in terms of his personal biography, my use of Whitehead's approach to analyze these works must go beyond iconographic readings that are capable of transforming singular elements into indelible signs. A Whiteheadian understanding of works such as *The Tearingness of Collaging* would emphasize the spaces between the individual parts, including all breaks, fissures, and gaps as being as important as the material components themselves. All these elements must be regarded, as the master process philosopher himself would recommend, as different force fields of energy giving rise to yet other forces in the intervening spaces separating them, rather than forming assembles of inert substances or representing only a biographical episode in the artist's life.

When embarking on a Whiteheadian interpretation of Motherwell's collage and painting aesthetic, one needs to look at how this artist sets up multiple disjunctions of non-cohering individual parts in his earliest collages rather than attempting to forge compelling unities from disconnected singularities as did such cubists as Picasso and such dadaists as Kurt Schwitters. "[T]he collagist," Motherwell explains, "takes a lot of disparate elements and places them. The problem is, given these disparate and conflicting elements, how ultimately to *unify* them. It's a painful and precarious way of making order. The separate elements tend to carry on guerrilla warfare with each other, a source of tension, true, but also possibly of chaos."[3]

Motherwell's innovative approach, which involves respecting the relative autonomy of each component in his work, is evident in one of his first collages, *Joy of Living* (1943). The title of this work resonates with Henri Matisse's *Le Bonheur de vivre* (1905–1906) in the Barnes Foundation, and this connection is noteworthy since Albert C. Barnes's monograph on Matisse was one of Motherwell's preferred sources when he first started to make art.[4] Motherwell's *Joy of Living* is perhaps more influenced by Barnes's description of the Matisse painting with this same title than the painting itself, particularly the following paragraph, which interprets Matisse's work as far more loosely composed than Barnes indicates elsewhere in his analysis of this work. Barnes writes:

What chiefly renders the movement is compositional interplay between the very numerous and variously shaped and placed lines and areas of color which constitute the pattern of the picture. The general linear flow is sometimes vertical…; sometimes horizontal…; but in most of the pattern the lines, with their conjoined area-lines, pass from one direction to another, and this change and alternation of direction pervades every part of the canvas. In conjunction with the diverse intervals between them, these compositionally active contour-lines lend a very great degree of variety to the space-motif, a variety which is augmented by differences in the sharpness of the outlines themselves, and the consequent differences in the movement suggested by them. As one plastic factor or another predominates, space becomes in turn shallow and deep, merely decorative or quite realistic, but always colorful, highly patterned, and full of compositional movement.[5]

An additional source is Motherwell's tremendous respect for Picasso's *The Studio* (1928) in the collection of art collector and gallerist Peggy Guggenheim, who opened in the fall of 1942 the New York gallery Art of This Century, which exhibited Motherwell's work. Max Ernst, who, as already noted, was friends with Motherwell, was briefly married to Guggenheim and had encouraged her to purchase this painting. Even as late as 1965, Motherwell remained enthusiastic about this work, saying, "My favorite picture in the whole Guggenheim collection was the white Picasso....I also loved a beautiful brown Miró."[6] The similarities between his *Joy of Life* and Picasso's *The Studio* are most apparent in the parallel use of a nested box-like configuration, which in the Picasso serves as an excuse for a full-length abstract painting of an equally abstract female prominently sited within the painting itself, thus extending the self-reflexive idea of one painting being used to picture another painting. While Motherwell perpetuated this type of *mise en abyme*, multiplying it several times over and even including the phallic triangle from Picasso's full-length portrait that punctures the central green ovoid in his own work, his collage evidences much more visual incidence than Picasso's painting.

This collage, with its two centralized magenta pieces of paper, now a faded pink, resembles the teeming and jostling world of Barnes's analysis of Matisse's *Le Bonheur de vivre*, even though it is comprised of different types of imagery, including a military training map, seemingly organic blobs, grids and frames, automatic gestures, and sets of web-like configurations. In creating this collage Motherwell avails himself of a rich assembly of mixed media, including oil, gouache, fabric, paper, crayon, charcoal, and ink on paperboard.[7] Working together, these figurative references and this wealth of media enunciate an intensely competitive world, articulated through tensions occasioned by very different velocities and temporalities. The respect Motherwell pays to the distinct character of each type of constituent making up this and other collages supports Whitehead's idea of beauty that depends on permitting each prehended element in an actual entity to maintain its original character even as it participates in the formation of such a concrescence. While each of the collaged elements in *Joy of Living* should ideally be able to be considered first as formal elements participating in an activated composition before accruing the different meanings society has ascribed to them, Whitehead rightly considers such "direct observation" to be an impossibility since cultural interpretations are intertwined with empirical looking and impact not only what is seen but also how it is viewed.[8]

While Motherwell's collage only slowly begins to come into focus as a distinct composition instead of a riotous conglomerate of competing geometric shapes and organic forms, its initial frenetic energy suggests a series of continued transformations. The jostling conjunctions and resulting tensions reinforce, with some irony, the vitality suggested by the work's title, an irony evident in the inevitable changes that have since occurred in some of the ephemeral materials comprising it—including brightly hued papers and some now faded papers, a number colored with German aniline dyes—that have impacted but not undermined the collage's more permanent status of being a work of art, thus enacting literally the theme of perpetual change. Moreover, this composition accords well with Whitehead's conclusion that beauty occurs when "the parts contribute to the massive feeling of the whole, and the whole contributes to the intensity of feeling of the parts,"[9] with the added proviso that the work be as fresh and spontaneous as an actual occasion since "Spontaneity, originality of decision, belongs to the essence of each actual occasion."[10]

Lest one consider this early work an anomaly in this artist's oeuvre, it is important to note that this same type of overloaded composition, encompassing a range of different competing elements, is found in another collage from the same year, *The Displaced Table*. This piece comprises a most unstill life, with its prominent nested black-and-white rectangle of spontaneously conceived gestures, resembling a precursive sketch for the *Elegies* Motherwell would initiate at the end of the decade. In this collage, a section of wood veneer, recalling cubist works with faux bois wallpaper, can also be understood as punning the conditional verb tense "would," making it a particularly appropriate Whiteheadian provisional (prehensive) element. The wood veneer looks as if it belongs to an incipient perspectival (illusionistic) realm, thereby pointing to an altogether different spatial dimension than the various cut, drawn, and painted two-dimensional shapes comprising the rest of the collage. The composition of precariously stacked forms making up *The Displaced Table* appears to be barely held together by the wire-like lines in the upper sections, even as the various individual elements in this collage seem to be struggling against one another, thereby presenting viewers with different tugging forces and dissimilar ways of being, ranging from the architectonic to the organic. The type of relational structure evident in this work is a precarious one, marked by unrelated, competing tensions, again bespeaking an array of jostling prehensive forces. From a Whiteheadian perspective the displacement signaled by this collage's title is indicative of the different velocities and temporalities that might be activated by prospective viewers to form new actual entities, i.e., interpretations.

The subject of becoming is transposed to "becoming other" in the important collage, *Pancho Villa, Dead and Alive*, made this same year and acquired by MoMA in 1944—a work that is similarly inspired by Picasso's *The Studio* in Peggy Guggenheim's collection. Because of this collage's insistent subject matter, I need to acknowledge the work's iconography as it impacts and interacts with the subdued yet notworthy forces setting up ongoing tensions in this work. A great deal has been written about this work, which was inspired by the assassination in 1923 of the Mexican Revolutionary General José Doroteo Arango Arámbula, better known as Francisco "Pancho" Villa. Because the collage shows only Villa's lower torso—naked with pink and alive genitals on the right and either covered with trousers or castrated on the left—even more attention needs to paid to the ways this piece permits very different readings. In addition to looking at the figure as dead and alive, as indicated in Motherwell's title, the two lower torsos can also be understood as dead and resurrected.

Pancho Villa, Dead and Alive is important not only for its revolutionary subject matter but also because it is one of the first décollages (a term meaning "to become unglued"), which was created six years before the innovative ripped and lacerated posters of French artists Jacques Villeglé and Raymond Hains that were made through excisions rather than additions to create images simulating the effects of weathering and vandalism on publicly displayed posters. Since the issue of subtraction is subsidiary to the main issue of addition in Motherwell's work, it is not surprising that his precedence in this important development in collage history has been overlooked. Where the figure of the dead and castrated Pancho Villa is located, Motherwell had originally placed a piece of paper. Traces of it still remain at the upper-left side and the lower-right edge of this area. Remnants of this sheet of paper reveal that the surface of this section was to be composed in alternating bands of gray and lemon yellow. Art historian E.A. Carmean has suggested that Motherwell originally intended to present an imprisoned figure in this section of the collage hence the title would have been *Pancho Villa: Free and Imprisoned*.[11]

There is a distinct irony evidenced in the choice of the German Christmas wrapping paper employed as the background for the right-hand side of *Pancho Villa, Dead and Alive* and a few other of this artist's collages of the mid-1940s, since its pulsating appearance implicitly refers to the war then being fought. This material also implies a Christian midwinter holiday, with its poetic resonances of rebirth during the darkest of seasons, while ostensibly directing viewers' attention to a hero of the Mexican 1910 Revolution. Comprised of spots of black superimposing a design of red foliate shapes resembling poinsettias, the paper can also be interpreted as referencing pointillism in general and French neoimpressionist Georges Seurat's work in particular, which was at the time of interest to Motherwell.[12] In addition, this wrapping paper in the context of Pancho Villa's assassination can be interpreted as an abstraction of destruction caused by bullet holes and blood. Motherwell remembered being especially moved by a photograph of the assassinated Pancho Villa showing the Mexican revolutionary sprawled across the seat of an automobile, the door of the car flung open and the lower portion of the torso prominently displayed, with the head thrown back almost out of view.[13] He may have thought he saw this particular image when he was in Mexico or in any one of the numerous histories of the revolution he read. However, photographs of the dead revolutionary show only the upper torso and outstretched arms of Pancho Villa's dead body hanging over a closed car door, not the lower torso depicted in Motherwell's collage, since he had evidently misremembered it. The collage is by turns hieratic, formal, and stoical as well as fluctuating and indicting of the revolution that is responsible for an execution-like murder and either an undressing or castration of this figure.

Motherwell's choice of this German Christmas wrapping paper functions as a particularly complex semiotic capable of communicating very different and even conflicting prehended energies. Considered from a Whiteheadian viewpoint, this type of paper can be prehended in a number of different ways, resulting in varied actual occasions, i.e., different works of art or, at the least, differing interpretations of this collage and thus divergent artworks. Instead of attempting to create highly formalist collages that bespeak a unified intentionality, Motherwell at this time opted for more open-ended creations with both chaotic and cohering contrapuntal rhythms capable of catalyzing a range of responses. However, his collages should not be construed as simply Rorschachs, serving as screens for the projection of any content a viewer might wish to ascribe to a given work. Over time Motherwell has denominated sets of meanings for the colors he most frequently uses such as black, white, red, and ochre. He also relies on associative titles, often with political and literary resonances, to serve as guides for his viewers.[14]

These three early collages can also be regarded as Motherwell's distinct contribution to the ongoing 1940s artistic discourse known as biomorphism (a neologism joining "bio," meaning life, and "morphism" referring to form). But Motherwell's biomorphism did limit his work to the mixture of abstracted unicellular forms working in concert with such cultural implements as the ancient and more recent tribal artifacts alluded to in the work of several of his fellow abstract expressionists during their formative years—a group including such painters as Krasner, Newman, Pollock, Richard Pousette-Dart, Rothko, and Theodoros Stamos. Instead, Motherwell's embrace of Whitehead's process philosophy enabled him to discern feelings across a wide spectrum of physical and biological sciences as well as popular cultural and artistic ephemera. In this way he was able to view his collage materials as replete with specific energies capable of evoking in his works a range of competing and also reinforcing feelings that encouraged him in turn to believe that his art was able to approximate the "felt quality" of the contemporary world. This belief in feelings being manifested by the conjunctions of his materials rather than somehow being caught up in his own emotions provided Motherwell with the opportunity to delegate more responsibility to them. As he did, his collages and paintings, occasionally in the 1950s and even more so in the 1960s, became increasingly minimal, resulting in the integral eloquence of their constituent media being given even greater and increasingly more powerful roles to play in his art.

Notes

1 In his fascinating study of Jackson Pollock's work, art historian Michael Schreyach takes Motherwell to task for his "identification of process with meaning" and suggests that Motherwell equates the meaning of his art solely with the process of making it rather than the final work of art. While Motherwell certainly does emphasize the process of working as my analysis of his use of Whiteheadian process philosophy intends to clarify, he also acknowledges on a number of occasions the intelligibility of the final work of art as both a record and a testament. A Whiteheadian actual entity both reflects the prehensive process giving rise to it as well as the satisfaction of achieving the completed state, the concrescence, represented by the work of art.

   Michael Schreyach, *Pollock's Modernism* (New Haven and London: Yale University Press, 2017).

2 Katy Rogers, "Chapter 5: Collages 1950–1957: The Tearingness of Collaging" in Jack Flam, Katy Rogers, and Tim Clifford, eds., *Robert Motherwell Paintings and Collages: A Catalogue Raisonné, 1941–1991*, Vol. 1 (New Haven: Yale University Press, 2012), p. 90.

3 Diamonstein, "An Interview with Robert Motherwell" in Arnason, ed., *Robert Motherwell*, p. 229.

4 Barnes and John Dewey were very close friends. Barnes's famous educational program was indebted to Dewey's educational approach, and Dewey dedicated his *Art as Experience* to Barnes. George E. Hein, "John Dewey and Albert C. Barnes: A Deep and Mutually Rewarding Friendship," *Dewey Studies* 1, No. 1 (Spring, 2017): 44–78.

   Motherwell was definitely influenced by Dewey's writings and referred to him from time to time, so his spirited embrace of Barnes's book may well have been with his full knowledge of the two men's long-term friendship and professional association.

5 Decades later, Motherwell recalled, "I read and reread Barnes long Matisse book. In fact, it was encrusted in oil paint when I finally gave it away." Robert Motherwell, "Letter to Bruce Grenville" (4 February 1982) in Terenzio, ed., *The Collected Writings of Robert Motherwell*, p. 249. Albert C. Barnes and Violette de Mazia, *The Art of Henri-Matisse* (Merion, PA: Barnes Foundation Press, 1933, rpt. 1963), p. 371.

6   Robert Motherwell, "Interview with Bryan Robertson, Addenda, 1965" in *The Collected Writings of Robert Motherwell*, p. 146.

7   Katy Rogers, "C 9: *Joy of Living*" in Jack Flam, Katy Rogers, and Tim Clifford, *Robert Motherwell Paintings and Collages: A Catalogue Raisonné, 1941–1991*, Vol. 3 (New Haven: Yale University Press, 2012), p. 3.

8   Whitehead's views of perception anticipate Merleau-Ponty's phenomenology, but he is more concerned with the ways culture imposes itself on sense perception. "In human experience," he writes, "the prehensions of the contemporary world exhibit themselves as sense-perceptions, effected by means of the bodily organs of sensation....But sense-perception, as conceived in the isolation of its ideal purity, never enters into human experience. It is always accompanied by so-called 'interpretation.'" Whitehead, *Adventures of Ideas*, p. 217.

9   Whitehead, *Adventures of Ideas*, p. 252.

10 Whitehead, *Adventures of Ideas*, p. 258.

11 E.A. Carmean, Jr., *The Collages of Robert Motherwell* (Houston: Museum of Fine Arts, Nov. 15, 1972—Jan. 14, 1973), p. 49.

12 In the well-known 1943 photograph of Motherwell seated in his studio, there is a reproduction of Seurat's *La Parade* on the wall, which was no doubt a favored work, as he had translated during his time in France (1938–1939) *D'Eugène Delacroix au Neo-Impressionisme* by Seurat's fellow neo-impressionist Paul Signac. According to Motherwell, his translation was lost at sea.

13 Robert Motherwell, Conversation with the Author, Greenwich, CT, March 28, 1975.

14 One of my favored pedagogical approaches since the 1970s has been to ask students at the beginning of a semester to select one work of art that they can study at first hand and then easily revisit so that they are able to write three to four short papers about different aspects of their chosen work by responding to a number of different questions that I pose. Near the end of the semester, when the students begin to bring together their research and insights into a final paper, they realize that the one work they have been investigating has become a series of overlapping and distinctly different ones. Thus, they recognize for themselves that the New Critical view attesting that all meanings inhere in a given work of art is a myth to be undermined, and that a work of art's intelligibility can be messaged and expanded. Employing this type of hermeneutical approach for my own research has enabled me to appreciate the openness of Motherwell's art to the perspectives of different viewers when approaching it.

6 Whitehead's Process and Susanne K. Langer's Symbol

Picasso's *The Studio* in Peggy Guggenheim's collection served as a paradigm for several of Motherwell's collages, beginning with his earliest works from 1943, as we have seen. This painting authorized one of Motherwell's predominant views of collage and painting as preeminent means for setting up relationships between one or more nested images inside a given artwork that in turn repeats its overall perimeter. In addition to this *mise en abyme*, gainsaid through reworking the compositional model provided by Picasso, Motherwell's collages enact an additional type of nesting, evidenced through each individual work's enclosure of two-dimensional and/or low-relief fragments from the outside world, at the same time these collages literally constitute, in their entirety, discrete bits of this much larger realm. This internal-external progression of nested forms is certainly one viable way to think about making collages, and it has proven to be an enduring tactic for Motherwell's contributions to this genre from 1943 until 1991 when he created his last ones. Moreover, since Motherwell objectified colors as things that he then disperses on canvas, his paintings are similarly involved in an internal/external dialectic.

There is a second favorite piece from Peggy Guggenheim's collection that has provided Motherwell with a different and equally rich prototype for thinking about collage and painting, and it is the aforementioned 1925 field painting by Miró, notable for its unevenly thinned brown painted background, punctuated with a few somewhat ambiguous figures and signs. Instead of using first the space inside a work's perimeter to reference an outside world, as the Picasso does, Miró's painting conjures up a totally separate universe, replete in itself, at the same time it includes in this realm several revealing figurative references.

Considered together, these two paintings provide very different aesthetic tactics that can be understood not only in terms of Picasso's and Miró's prototypes but also in relation to Whitehead's work and that of his former graduate student Susanne K. Langer, who completed her 1926 dissertation, "A Logical

Analysis of Meaning," under his direction. The first model, based on the Picasso painting, parallels Whitehead's view of concrescing forces, which he has characterized, as noted earlier, in terms of "the throbbing emotion of the past hurling itself into a new transcendent fact," to describe first the creation of the actual entity, which I have regarded as the art object itself, before becoming a source for the next stage of actual entities resulting from each individual viewer's interaction with a given work. Differing from Picasso's precedence, the Miró model might be understood as paralleling the basic contradictions that are formative for Langer's thought. She considers artworks to be meaningful in terms of the r*epresentational logic* of comparative analogies or metaphors, which she has defined in terms of "saying one thing and meaning another, and expecting to be understood to mean the other"[1] and *presentational symbols*, whereby the work of art presents its own meaning directly as a qualitative whole, a type of gestalt, with each component "involved in a simultaneous integral presentation."[2]

Langer first met Whitehead in 1924 soon after he arrived in the United States from London, where he had retired from the position of Chief Professor of Mathematics at the University of London's Imperial College of Science and Technology in order to join Harvard's philosophy department. Whitehead came to Harvard with a most impressive reputation for having coauthored the *Principia Mathematica* as well as having written other books on philosophy and education. A graduate student at Radcliffe, Langer asked Whitehead to be her dissertation adviser even though her topic on logic seemed more in line with his earlier work with Russell and appeared to be further removed from his present metaphysical research.

To acquaint herself with Whitehead's recent thinking, Langer attended his graduate seminar on metaphysics in which he was developing ideas for the series of prestigious Gifford Lectures, which he delivered at the University of Edinburgh during the 1927-1928 session—and later published as *Process and Reality*, one of his major and most challenging works. After receiving her PhD, Langer invited Whitehead to write a preface for her 1930 book *The Practice of Philosophy*. Twelve years later she dedicated her first major work in aesthetics entitled *Philosophy in a New Key: A Study in the Symbolism of Reason, Rite, and Art* to Whitehead, whom she referred to as "my great Teacher and Friend," although she pointed out in her preface that "the writings of the sage to whom this book is dedicated receive but scant explicit mention."[3] Even when she was a graduate student working with Whitehead, Langer found Ernst Cassirer's *The Philosophy of Symbolic Forms*, which she had read in German, much more useful for her work. In her published research Langer rarely mentions Whitehead's name, and her involvement in the logic of symbolic forms would suggest great differences from his work.

Until the late 1990s, philosophers tended to discount any reliance Langer might have had on Whitehead's process philosophy. Fortunately, philosophers Randall Auxier, Donald Dryden, and Rolf Lachmann discerned Langer's connections with Whitehead's process theories, and their reevaluation resulted in the special 1997 issue of *Process Studies* which Lachmann edited.[4] More recently, Adrienne Dengerink Chaplin has written *The Philosophy of Susanne Langer: Embodied Meaning in Logic, Art and Feeling.* In her book, Chaplin states:

> Langer was immensely influenced by Whitehead's thinking. This applies not only to his *Principia Mathematica* but to all his subsequent philosophical work, whether on science, perception, process or education.[5]

One of the main reasons I view Langer's work as a necessary contribution to my investigation of Motherwell and Whitehead is that her theories about the overall work of art as a presentational symbol help clarify the way Whitehead's prehensive forces (his relational structures) function in artworks. For Langer, symbols differ substantially from signs: whereas signs only point to their referents, symbols are experiential in providing qualitative human perspectives through which individual artworks can be conceived and understood, so that works of art not only present special qualitative contents but just as importantly they also provide the lens for appreciating and understanding these distinct meanings.[6]

Citing one of Langer's unpublished manuscripts in his essay for the special issue of *Process Studies*, Dryden emphasizes her characterization of Whiteheadian metaphysics as "a strange creation by a great scientist" before qualifying this assessment. She does so by comparing Whitehead's work to other great metaphysical systems in "go[ing] beyond the inventor's literal conception" in order to constitute "a genuine philosophic myth—not an allegory or consciously poetic statement, but a living myth, intended as literal truth."[7] Ironically this view of groundbreaking philosophy as first a myth before becoming a rationally organized system is a theory Whitehead himself entertained, as I indicated earlier, so even Langer's evaluation of Whitehead's work can be likened to a criterion he articulated. In her introductory textbook *The Practice of Philosophy*, Langer historicizes philosophy as developing periodically over time through the introduction of such myths or overarching metaphors—we might consider them in terms of Thomas Kuhn's later formulation of paradigm shifts—which are capable of setting up major changes in people's way of thinking:

> Such a discovery reorientates [sic] our whole world. It gives rise to a new outlook in philosophy, and in its time is apt to be hailed as the very

Truth, the insight which reveals the whole secret of Being….[Such a set of originally intuited insights] must, in its original form, be regarded as a myth, which sets forth freshly and naively some new point of view… [while providing] new opportunities for rational construction."[8]

Langer's assessment is entirely in sync with Whitehead's own view of "the leap of imagination reach[ing] beyond the safe limits of the epoch, and beyond the safe limits of learned rules of taste…[to produce] the dislocations and confusions marking the advent of new ideals for civilized effort."[9]

Because of her respect for Whitehead as an original thinker, Langer has taken some of his ideas, mainly prehensive elements concrescing into actual entities, and personalized them so that they accord with the logic of artistic symbols, even at the expense of reifying them. Since logic and later aesthetics are her prime subjects, Langer needed to redirect Whitehead's process theory so that it was able to describe how works of art function. "I do not hold what is known as an 'expressionist' theory of art," Langer has written, summarizing the route she took in *Philosophy in a New Key*, as she also was rethinking Whitehead's view of feelings as energizing forces giving rise to a perpetually changing world. Instead, she wrote of "regard[ing] artistic expression of feelings as a logical expression, not a venting of emotions."[10]

By logical expression, Langer is referring to her new key—relational feelings—referenced in the title of her book, which she discusses in terms of music. Her new key is an abstraction; it moves beyond a simple outburst of emotions to structured realizations enabling them to be conceived in the work of art, and feelings taken from life are reconstituted as sets of analogies or metaphoric relations that can then be articulated as patterns of feeling in art on the basis of a common structure, which often takes the form of an analogy (simile) or metaphor that both share. As Langer points out in *The Practice of Philosophy*, "the expressiveness of any thing which functions as a symbol depends upon its logical structure….Moreover, the symbolic relation between any two things holds just in so far as the two things are analogous."[11] For one thing to symbolize another thing, one or more elements in the first thing must correspond to one or more aspects found in the second one. To illustrate this point, Langer makes her famous pattern-and-suit analogy:

> Whenever we know that two systems exemplify the same pattern, we know that any essential configuration in one system will find its analogue in the other; just as the lines and proportions of a suit are analogous to those of its paper prototype. Therefore, any alternation or combination that can be made in the one system can also be made in the other….Thus any logical construct in a system can be *expressed* by an analogous logical construct in any other system having the same form.[12]

Langer's pattern-and-suit analogy can be used to explain her view of artistic form's modus operandi—the pattern itself—which she regards as a relational structure and an overarching symbol that often subsumes under its auspices conventional symbols. Conventional symbols or signs in the Miró field painting mentioned earlier operate at a different semantic level than his superintending symbol, the painting in toto as a primary type of feeling gestalt. One of his sign systems consists of the abstract signs for a male in the upper left, another is used for the female represented in the center, and a third is connoted by the yellow flame in the lower right, which might signify love or passion. These signs evince structural and metaphorical relationships to traditional signs for masculine rationality (the sun) and female sexuality (the curvaceous figure "8"), both taking place on an earth-colored brown field. The formal system under which this group of painted signs is subsumed serves as the overarching symbol constituting the work of art that in turn qualifies each of the conventional signs found in it. In other words, the painting as symbol constitutes the *lens* through which this work and its various components are to be understood. In consideration of Motherwell's interest in this painting by Miró, I suggest that he was engaged with Whitehead's process theory when considering his collages as constellations of different energies and also with Langer when considering how art as a presentational symbol, i.e., a relational structure, can itself be an analogous form of cognition about the world.

When Langer takes Whitehead's theory of actual entities as relational structures and redirects it to formulate her view of symbols in the visual arts and in music as nonverbal types of understanding, her work helps Motherwell crystallize his own thoughts about how abstract works of art can serve as modes of cognition. He does this most empathically in 1963 when he analogizes his own relationship with his chosen artistic media in terms of love—thereby joining aspects of Whitehead's and Langer's philosophy in his own work:

> Now, if a creative person in the arts is a person with an extraordinary capacity for love…he therefore directs his love toward the other thing in human existence as rich, sensitive, supple and complicated as human beings themselves; that is to say toward an artistic medium, which is not an inert object, or conversely, a set of rules for composition, but a living collaboration, which not only reflects every nuance of one's being, but which, in the moments in which one is lost, comes to one's aid not arbitrarily and capriciously…, but seriously, accurately, concretely *with you*, as when a canvas says to you: this empty space in me needs to be pinker; or a shape says: I want to be larger and more expansive; or the format says: the conception is too large or too small for me, all out of scale; or a stripe says: gouge me more—you are too polite and elegant; or a gray says: a bit more blue—my present tone is uncomfortable and does not fit with what surrounds me.[13]

Like Whitehead, Langer regards feelings in art as analogous structures enabling them to be envisioned, a stance that might seem to erode the power of its presence (her representational logic). But, in a contradictory fashion, she also joins this substitutive and analogical situation with the power of art as a formal gestalt (her presentational symbol). She does this in order to maintain the centrality of art's occurrence, an approach not unlike Miró's painting in Peggy Guggenheim's collection in maintaining its status as first and foremost a discrete and separate entity before one looks more closely for the formative analogies and metaphors giving rise to the abstract personages inhabiting this special alternative world. In *Philosophy in a New Key*, Langer concludes with a gestaltist view of art as a wholistic and integrated presentation:

The meanings of all other symbolic elements that compose a larger, articulate symbol are understood only through the meaning of the whole, through their relations within the total structure. Their very functioning as symbols depends on the fact that they are involved in a simultaneous, integral presentation. This kind of semantic may be called "presentational symbolism," to characterize its essential distinction from discursive symbolism, or "language" proper.[14]

To the concept of art as a presentational symbol, a formal and conceptual gestalt, Motherwell responded circuitously in his public lecture entitled "Symbolism," which he delivered at Hunter College in 1954:

But the symbolic thought is *in* the work, so to speak, and not *about* it; otherwise you would be thinking a symbolizing of a symbolizing, not merely symbolizing. I do not think it is possible to do both at once. At least I have never had a thought about painting while painting, but only afterwards. In this sense one can only think *in* painting while holding a brush before a canvas, and this symbolization I trust much more than the thinking that I do *about painting all day long.*[15]

Even earlier, in the transcript for a lecture given in 1949, but never published, Motherwell responds more directly to Langer's theories; in fact, he quotes at length from her *Philosophy in a New Key* to elucidate the way in which meaning can inhere in a work of art. This selection of passages from Langer's text is used to explain how symbols can be understood as a form of meaningful communication different from everyday speech. Motherwell held Langer's explications of the ways symbols function in the highest esteem "as some of the most moving passages in modern philosophy."[16] He points out that she posits two current epistemological assumptions (1) "that language is the only means of articulating thought, and (2) "that everything that is not speakable thought, is feeling." If both these assumptions are true, he then hypothesizes that large portions of human experience might not be able to be communicated; however, he takes note of Langer's theory that every language has a vocabulary and syntax and is capable of translation from one language to another. In verbal languages some words are equivalent to other words and also to combinations of them; meanings can be expressed in many ways. But nonverbal languages like painting and music do not share these characteristics. Motherwell cites Langer's following statement, "They [symbols in art and music] have neither words nor syntax nor a dictionary, nor are capable of equivalent translation into another language, nor are they capable of generalizing, as words do." According to Motherwell, Langer is affirming that the work of art is "first and foremost a direct presentation of an individual object," which can be used to formulate symbols, whose elements are "involved in a simultaneous, integral presentation" and whose meanings are determined, as noted earlier, by their relation within the art-works' overarching structure, which they in turn support. Langer character-izes this type of symbolism, as noted earlier, as presentational to distinguish it from the discursive type or language proper. To reinforce Langer's concept, Motherwell includes the following quotation from her *Philosophy in a New Key* in his talk:

> The recognition of presentation symbolism as a normal and prevalent vehicle of meaning widens our conception of rationality far beyond the widest boundaries, yet never breaks faith with logic in the strictest sense. Whenever a symbol operates, there is meaning; and conversely, different classes or experience—say, reason, intuition, appreciation—correspond to different types of symbolic meditation. No symbol is exempt from the office of logical formulation, of *conceptualizing* what it conveys; how-ever simple its import, or however great, this import is a meaning, and therefore an element for understanding.

Motherwell then cites Langer's statement pertaining to her conviction that such a method would bring "within the compass of reason much that has been traditionally relegated to 'emotion,' or to that crepuscular depth of the mind where 'intuitions' are supposed to be born." Her statement provides him with a theoretical basis for believing feeling can be given symbolic form in his art because symbols are definite forms of communication and accrue meaning from the relations of the elements composing them. Motherwell highlights the following conclusion from Langer's argument:

> If all thinking is fundamentally symbolizing, language is a different kind of symbolizing from painting; the relational structure that each represents is different in kind; and consequently expresses different

meaning relations, i.e., the meanings best expressed in words cannot be communicated in painting, nor can painting meanings be converted into words.

When symbols are regarded in this way, he concludes, painters do think in very definite and articulate ways, even though they think in painting terms, not in words:

> The curse of a painter's existence is that he lives in a verbal society, and is consequently supposed to be articulate. If you people could only guess the worlds of meaning that cannot be said in words, that we are able to articulate in painting every day!

Motherwell summarizes his conviction that paintings can function as articulate symbols, and an artist's most important thoughts are not verbal, even though they may incorporate words. Speaking analogously, one could hypothesize that colors and shapes are Motherwell's vocabulary, the relational structures are his syntax, the brush his voice, and he himself a conduit, all of which work in unison to present "feelings, the expression of the world as felt." In this phrase Motherwell is referring not only to his own feelings but also to the feeling/energy expressed by his media; the conflation of the two form integrated structures, which he equates with symbolic thinking.

While Motherwell's analysis of symbolic thought in the visual arts demonstrates his endorsement of Langer's presentational symbolism, as my analysis suggests, it also depends on Whitehead's view of prehending feelings or vectors of energy stemming from the world, the artist, the act of creating itself, and the actual entity that is being formed through the concrescence of these forces, all of them coming together in the process of creation. One can conclude that Motherwell was well enough versed in Whitehead's view of creative dynamics as a basis for the universe and Langer's consideration of artistic symbols as modes of thinking to join the two: Whitehead's theories thus enabled him to think about the creative process, while Langer's explications, provided him with a way to comprehend how his nondiscursive work can communicate on different semantic levels: first, as founding an overall symbolic or emotional gestalt, and second, as functioning similar to metaphors by representing distinct iconographic forms.

Notes

1 Susanne K. Langer, *The Problems of Art: Ten Philosophical Lectures* (New York: Charles Scribner's Sons, 1957), p. 23.
2 Susanne K. Langer, *Philosophy in a New Key* (Cambridge: Harvard University Press, 1967), p. 97.

3 Susanne K. Langer, "Preface to the First Edition," in *Philosophy in a New Key*, p. xv.
4 *Process Studies*, special Issue: Langer and Alfred North Whitehead, ed. Rolf Lachmann, 26 (1997).
5 Chaplin, *The Philosophy of Susanne Langer: Embodied Meaning in Logic, Art and Feeling*, pp. 100–101.
6 Langer, *Philosophy in a New Key*, p. 61.
7 Donald Dryden, "Whitehead's Influence on Susanne Langer's Conception of Living Form," *Process Studies* 26, No. 1–2 (1997): 62–85, http://www.anthonyfl ood.com/drydenlangerwhitehead.htm, consulted 5 April 2018.
8 Susanne K. Langer, *The Practice of Philosophy* (New York: Henry Holt and Company, Inc., 1930), pp. 173 and 178.
9 Whitehead, "Adventures of Ideas," p. 279.
10 Susanne K. Langer, "Reply to Henry Aiken's Criticism," *Philosophy and Phenomenological Research* 7. No. 4 (June, 1947): 672.
11 Langer, *The Practice of Philosophy*, p. 115.
12 Langer, *The Practice of Philosophy*, p. 99.
13 Robert Motherwell, "'A Process of Painting" (5 October 1963) in Terenzio, ed., *The Collected Writings of Robert Motherwell*, p. 139.
14 Langer, *Philosophy in a New Key*, p. 97.
15 Robert Motherwell, "'Symbolism," Lecture presented at Hunter College, New York City, 24 February 1954. Ashton and Banach, eds., *The Writings of Robert Motherwell*, p. 170.
16 Robert Motherwell, Transcript of Untitled Lecture on Susanne K. Langer and Visual Thinking, c. 1949, n.p. All the quotations included in the following discussion of Motherwell and Langer are taken from this transcript.

7   Conclusion
Material Means, Immaterial Results

My investigation of both Motherwell's collage aesthetic and abstract expressionism's connections with Whitehead's process philosophy points to the heretofore unexamined theoretical underpinnings that connect this art to quantum physics, which was formative to Whitehead's origination of organism, its process-oriented and humanistic counterpart. "Art," this theorist concluded, "at its highest exemplifies the metaphysical doctrine of the interweaving of absoluteness upon relativity."[1] His approach enabled him to theorize reality in terms of the dynamism of perpetual becoming, predicated on fields of prehending energies. Instead of static substances, these self-generating constellations briefly concresce into actual entities before they are prehended into other actual occasions in a process of never-ending creativity as existence's decisive principle. When considered in terms of the ongoing vitality of Whitehead's systems, Motherwell's collages deemphasize their cubist and dadaist counterparts' insistent materiality in favor of the diverse energies his works articulate. Viewed in this Whiteheadian manner, his collages and his overall collage aesthetic serve as the basis for a new way of thinking about his works in particular and abstract expressionist paintings in general. Thus, these works are as far-reaching in their revisionism as Pollock's drip paintings, Willem de Kooning's women, Rothko's veils, and Newman's zips, since these artists' paintings, including Motherwell's, articulate, albeit in distinctly individual ways, force fields of energy.

As my study of Motherwell's work and thought has set out to demonstrate, not only were Whitehead's ideas about process metaphysics vital for him and his theorization of his own art, but they—or Motherwell's summaries of them—appear to have been crucial factors in abstract expressionism's genesis. Motherwell's possibly unconscious distillation of Whitehead's theories in the form of plastic automatism became one significant conduit for their dissemination, which took the place of direct encounters with this philosopher and his writings. In the 1940s when Motherwell proselytized the enormous benefits of plastic automatism to several abstract expressionists, he subtly transformed, as I have suggested, this surrealist technique to accord with his understanding of process philosophy, which had become a foundational perspective for thinking about art and life.

The intensity with which Motherwell shared his ideas, and the strength of his fellow artists' responses are evident in his account of an early meeting with Pollock:

> I remember that Baziotes called up Pollock and we made a date to go and spent a whole afternoon with him. I talked, I guess, for four or five hours explaining the whole surrealist thing in general and the theory of automatism in particular, which nowadays we would call a technique of free association. I showed Pollock how Klee and Masson made their things, etc. And Pollock to my astonishment, listened intently; in fact, he invited me to come back another afternoon, which I did. This would be the winter of 1942.[2]

Even taking into consideration Motherwell's penchant for self-aggrandizement, as well as the fact that Pollock would unquestionably have been familiar with the work of Klee and Masson as well as the surrealists' use of psychic automatism, this future drip painter was obviously intrigued with Motherwell's personalization and transformation of this surrealist theory as well as the generosity with which he shared his ideas and learning.

In addition to transposing the relevancy of postclassical physics and Whiteheadian process metaphysics into the technique of plastic automatism for abstract expressionism's gestural wing, I am also suggesting its significance for the color field paintings of Rothko and his close associate Newman, especially since Motherwell has gone on record as sharing his ideas about this type of automatism with Rothko.[3] The following thoughtful discussion of Newman's paintings by the eminent twentieth-century British curator and critic Lawrence Alloway is supportive of this position:

> His [Newman's] field is holistic, but phased, like, say, the phases of the moon, parts of one movement. The exhilarating or ominous all-over color of Newman's paintings are not simply sensational. On the contrary, the color embodies an act of order. Such a continuous plane like a magnetic or electric field in physics, contains all potential force within it and it is important to bear in mind that an order of this nature is implicit in Newman's art. He presents the field and its phased modification, both as a finite visual image and as a statement of continuous potential order.[4]

While Alloway dwells on energy, physics, and forces *in potentia* when discussing Newman's work, Whitehead looks at prehended feelings, the culminating force of concrescence, and actual entities as ontological truths. With his personal knowledge of Whitehead and intense investment in his ideas, Motherwell elevates feeling—predicated on relationships of energy in a given work—above knowledge. As he concludes, "Knowledge never solves a picture: it depends on feeling," before elaborating, "Knowledge by itself can lead one to fake feeling—which other painters instantly recognize....An artist is someone who has an abnormal sensitivity to a medium."[5]

Because of misconstruing art's feeling for artists' emotions, art writers have regarded the abstract expressionists, including Motherwell, as being the last romantics, who culminated a tradition initiated in late eighteenth-century Germany. However, these paintings are far removed from beliefs in the direct transcription of the heart's sentiments into artistic form that some early romantics espoused. Members of the New York School were able to advance beyond a straightforward expression of their emotions as they adopted automatist techniques that enabled them to move from intuitive sketches to energized relationships and then to works of art predicated on a range of velocities. In this way they were able to create paintings capable of registering prehended—process orienting—forces; in other words, they achieved different forms of abstraction based on the overarching principle of first improvisation followed by distinctly individual emphases. This art is of course highly material in terms of the roles played by its constituent media, particularly oil paint, which Baziotes subjected to opalescent glazes in his later work, de Kooning slathered on his canvases in competing brushstrokes, Clyfford Still appeared to excoriate in his broad fields, Krasner furred in her *Umber and White* series, Motherwell objectified as pieces of color, Newman contrasted between unitary fields and loosely brushed edges, Pollock dripped, Pousette-Dart rendered in staccato-like dabs, and Rothko transformed into massive blocks of powdery pigment. Altogether abstract expressionism's focus on contingent relationships forged between dynamic and often contending forces, creating ongoing tensions and contrapuntal rhythms, undermines the idea that inert and simply material substances rather than perceptible interactions of energy are these works' main subject. Their work can be characterized in the same way Whitehead summarized Shelley's poem "The Cloud" as revealing "the endless, eternal elusive change of things."[6]

In this present study focusing on a tripartite investigation of Motherwell, philosophy, and art, I am suggesting that Whitehead's process theories be added to the canon of espoused concepts that are crucial for the development and understanding of abstract expressionism. I do so even though most adherents of this loosely affiliated group would be very surprised to see their names linked to his theories and might well question associations between quantum physics and their own work. However, one of the gratifications of being a historian is the possibility of discerning patterns that people in a given period were too close to their actual circumstances to see, and the present study hopefully belongs to this type of retrospective investigation. As I have set out to demonstrate, Motherwell's grounding in Whitehead's metaphysics enabled him to transform surrealist psychic automatism from an individually driven art to one in which artists and their media play codeterminative roles. It also enabled him to communicate these ideas to his fellow artists who became prominent abstract expressionists. In this way Motherwell's interpretation of Whitehead's ideas has indirectly contributed to this art's enhanced view of the media's formative role and the ensuing ongoing tensions between vital forces that have enabled this work to be analyzed as painted and collaged force fields of energy and related to one of the twentieth-century's great scientific discoveries, quantum mechanics. As the abstract expressionist with the most formal training in philosophy, Motherwell became a recognized apologist for the group. However, some of his most significant contributions, as I have indicated, come early in abstract expressionism's history as an important set of generative concepts on which this work is predicated, not just later when he proposes "New York School" as a stylistic designation for the group. Considering both Motherwell and abstract expressionism in this way, I believe that we are now equipped to see how Whitehead, one of the premier thinkers of the first half of the twentieth century, whose process metaphysics, which was profoundly influenced by quantum theory and was predicated on the inherent and ongoing creativity of the universe, played such a significant role in abstract expressionism's genesis and continued relevance.[7]

Notes

1   Whitehead, *Adventures of Ideas*, p. 264.
2   Motherwell, "Interview with Sidney Simon: 'Concerning the Beginnings of the New York School: 1939–1943" in Terenzio, ed., *The Collected Writings of Robert Motherwell*, p. 161.
3   Motherwell, "Interview with Sidney Simon: 'Concerning the Beginnings of the New York School: 1939–1943" in Terenzio, ed., *The Collected Writings of Robert Motherwell*, p.166. Motherwell pointed out,

> When he [Rothko] developed the style in the late 1940s for which he is now famous, he told me that there was always automatic drawing under those larger forms....And of course it was Pollock who became the most identified with this technique of working. In his dripping, one could see most clearly and nakedly the essential nature of the process.

4   Lawrence Alloway, "Barnett Newman," *Artforum* 3 (June, 1965): 20.
5   Motherwell, "Robert Motherwell: A Conversation at Lunch" (November, 1962) in Terenzio, ed., *The Collected Writings of Robert Motherwell*, p. 135.

6 The line Whitehead cites is "I change but I cannot die." Whitehead, *Science and the Modern World*, p. 86.
7 This relevance can include recent attempted ecological solutions that are analogous to abstract expressionism in searching for ways to structure and balance, however precariously, the chaos of the many different types of forces assaulting the twenty-first-century world.

Appendix A: Metaphors as Whiteheadian Prehensive Tools

The following essay was presented as a paper in 2010 for a symposium held in conjunction with Ann Tempkin's exhibition "Abstract Expressionism at The Museum of Modern Art." Since that time, I have reworked it by taking into consideration my research on Whitehead.

I now wish to extend my investigation of Motherwell's art by looking more closely at how metaphor, which in process philosophy can be considered as a type of prehensive tool resulting in an actual entity of concrescing forces, results in a momentary and also novel consolidation of them. Specifically, I will be looking at parallels between the metaphors in Motherwell's daily conversation, which serve as expository tools, and those found in his art that function spatially as framing devices for setting up and crossing boundaries. The goal is to understand how metaphors in Motherwell's art enact a way of thinking about the in-between realm, the metaxis his art sets up as a proposition and implicitly questions.

In consideration of this goal, let me say that I have always admired French poet Paul Valéry's c. 1930's response to Stéphane Mallarmé's visual poem "A Throw of Dice" ("Un Coup de Dés") (1897), when he wrote, "It seemed to me that I was looking at the form and pattern of a thought, placed for the first time in finite space. Here space itself truly spoke, dreamed, and gave birth to temporal forms. Expectancy, doubt, consternation, all were *visible* things."[1] In order to suggest a similar capability for Motherwell's art to figure thought, I will consider his collage and painting aesthetic in relation to both metaphor and artificial intelligence. This approach will enable me to pinpoint the way his art functions dialectically like Mallarmé's " A Throw of Dice" by seesawing between those elements traditionally inside the work and the realm outside it so that the art appears to jump boundaries and, in the course of doing so, enables one frame to critique the other.

My approach parallels Gilles Deleuze's opposition in *Difference and Repetition*[2] between encounters and established representations. Deleuze regards genuine encounters as ruptures to accepted ways of responding that make us think, while representations merely confirm a status quo. When art functions as an encounter, predicated on movements from internal to external frames, it simulates artificial intelligence's most notable quest: the creation of a system capable of moving outside itself in order to critique itself. While artificial intelligence experts can write programs with inclusive critiques, they remain at the cusp of being able to create programs that innovate new modes of assessment by moving outside their preordained systems in order to assess them.

A notable example of Motherwell's metaphoric thinking took place during my first conversation with him in the fall of 1974. In the course of our conversation, I mentioned being at first being puzzled by a handwritten reference, found in his personal archives, where decades earlier he had left it, without any explanation, an intriguing solitary reference to a pool of ambergris lying on the surface of the ocean. I explained to Motherwell that I had begun to think about how this isolated fragment could be considered a particularly apt metaphor for his paintings and some of his collages. Ambergris, a solid waxy substance produced in the intestines of sperm whales and used as a fixative for perfume, I reasoned, could be analogized in terms of paint. During our conversation, Motherwell confirmed that he indeed thought about painting in this metaphorical way.[3] While this exchange indicates Motherwell's reactions to his art, it also suggests how the metaphors occurring in his work—that is paintings or collages enacting the ruptures of the *mise en abyme* mentioned in reference to the Picasso in the Peggy Guggenheim collection—can function as a metaxis, an in-between reality, for viewers.

I came to know Motherwell much better during the academic year of 1975–1976 when I lived in his Greenwich, CT, guesthouse while teaching at Yale. The ensuing familiarity with his daily life enabled me to see how he would grasp hold of aspects of the world in terms of the analogies he continually devised in the course of conversing, an approach indicative of a desire to find specific and concrete felt responses to the world around him. He employed similes and metaphors as ongoing modes of apperception not only to understand a given topic but also to comprehend a way of doing so. Although metaphors certainly displace meaning, they also establish the possibility for intriguing alliances by establishing bridges between one's thoughts and the world, thus serving as the basis for new insights, so that in Whiteheadian fashion one might entertain the idea that the metaphor takes hold and prehends Motherwell rather than the reverse, as has been the case traditionally when the artist is assumed to be synonymous with the role of form giver rather the person who is formed through the auspices of particularly apt metaphors. This prehensive reversal is particularly true in art, where the second term of a comparison can be reversed in significance and become a primary means of identification. As an example, the framing elements in many Motherwell collages and the u-shaped configuration found in his *Open* series, begun in the late 1960s, can be understood as creating a rhyme between internal and external frames to the point that the internal figure supplants and dominates the external perimeters of a given work. Metaphors for Motherwell were a means of "emphasis" and also a manner of thinking as a "transaction between contexts," to use literary theorist I.A. Richards's felicitous phrase, based on rewarding comparisons enabling access to abstract ideas through familiar means.[4]

Long before George Lakoff and Mark Johnson theorized metaphors in their book *Metaphors We Live By*[5] as primary spatial and substantive means for grasping hold of the world and subsuming humans under their auspices, Motherwell's more poetic metaphors that peppered his conversations served as prehensile tools, joining discrete aspects of the work while collaboratively and briefly creating new dynamic syntheses. Successful metaphors, of course, work dialectically by comparing an established term with another one, and together they prehend a newly realized connection becoming novel actual entities. The two components also can be said to come together while also maintaining the break between them, thereby preserving the privilege of both shared and separate identities.

I would now like to return to the goal of connecting Motherwell's paintings to the figurative speech in his daily conversation. To do this, I will rely on Douglas R. Hofstadter's examination of artificial intelligence in his *Gödel, Escher, Bach: An Eternal Golden Braid*,[6] a book with which Motherwell was most likely unfamiliar. The reason for citing this text is to enable us to look at Motherwell's visual metaphors as operating in a manner similar to Hofstadter's strange loops or tangled hierarchies, particularly their ability to transgress limits and cross boundaries. One way to envisage a strange loop is to think of oneself walking on a Möbius strip, an activity that would enable one to be both inside and outside this imaginary thoroughfare at the same time, a situation Hofstadter is careful to underscore through an analysis of Maurits Cornelis Escher's *Picture Gallery*. In Escher's 1956 lithograph, a surrogate viewer gazes at a work of art in a gallery, which morphs into an overall city scene that in turn encompasses this young male observer, so the seer is also seen, and this interactive process constitutes a diagram of a type of prehensive and concrescing process.

I contend that a consideration of metaphors as strange loops enables us to understand the modus operandi of several Motherwell series, particularly his decades-long painterly discursus on the disjunctive themes of window and wall, a subject which he inherited from a number of sources, including Mallarmé's poetry and Matisse's painting, and a thematic appearing in many collages that play on the opposing ideas of openness and closure. Significant for Motherwell and his notable reliance on flat, two-dimensional surfaces in his painting was Mallarmé's early sonnet *"Les Fenêtres"* where the windows referenced in the title hold out promises of idealized transcendence while their very real and immanent, two-dimensional panes mirror the hospital room to which its condemned patient/inmate is incarcerated.

In addition to their resonances with these and other poems, metaphors in Motherwell's paintings function in much the same way as Mallarmé's series of fan poems, which were written on actual fans, inscribed and painted with decorations by the poet, to be presented as gifts to a few close female friends as well as to his wife Maria and daughter Geneviève. In both these fan poems and Motherwell's paintings and collages, there is an ongoing dynamic of unfolding and refolding, a flickering of release and closure, simulating both figuratively and formally the dynamics of thought, which readers and viewers might enact as they follow the traceries of allusions and references found in these works. Mallarmé's fan poem for his wife Maria enacts a visual and verbal rhyming between the actual fan on which the poem was inscribed and the cadenced beating of a young bird's wings, while many of Motherwell's collages, particularly his later painterly ones, are comprised of decisive and seemingly spontaneously conceived marks on mostly monochromatic fields. In collages or paintings, such as the *Opens*, which play on nested imagery, the internal rectangles reenact the paintings' restraining edges, at times appearing even to have been extracted from them, inspired by them, or totally separated from them, so their enclosing perimeters appear to be preserved within the works themselves, thereby establishing contrapuntal and contradictory rhythms, predicated on the dynamics of openness and closure.

Inside Motherwell's work, whether it be painting, collage, or print media, there is a shift analogous to Mallarmé's observation in the "Preface" to "A Throw of Dice" about the material's intervention, thus setting up strategic oscillating movements between a given work's material components and its subject matter. In this situation, the art's dynamic oscillation between form and figure participates in a situation whereby the work appears to be reflecting on itself and its means of communicating through both its abstract form and its status as a culture artifact, in other words, figuring thought. In this situation, collages, when considered solely in terms of themselves, bespeak a consciousness or thought of an absolute realm beyond the temporality and contingency connoted by the integrative process and its appropriated fragments from the external world.

As well as this contrapuntal movement between material and subject, there is also the possibility of rethinking many of Motherwell's works, particularly his *Open* paintings volumetrically in terms of full and empty when one compares them to Mallarmé's "Funeral Toast (To Théophile Gautier)" ["Toast Funèbre (à Théophile Gautier)"] in which the poem in its entirety is metaphorized as an empty glass, raised in homage to this once famous mid-nineteenth-century French Parnassian poet but only able to toast him figuratively and indirectly since it is essentially self-reflexive, i.e., mirroring itself and its own means of being reproduced.

Besides serving as an operative mode for the *Open* series, the idea of moving both inside and outside Motherwell's art through the counterpoint of nested imagery or openness and closure is also a working premise for many of Motherwell's collages and for his overall reliance on the collage aesthetic in his paintings. In these works Motherwell's viewers are encouraged to consider, literally and figuratively, both internal and external positions. Significantly, neither the internal nor the external positions are conclusive viewer stances; the two proffered roles are dynamic and interactive opportunities: each is connected with its opposite to create, by turns, an enfolding and alienating atmosphere, consequent with collage's mode of enacting thought—its consciousness of itself as an in-between process, caught in the present, yet pointing like metaphors to a realm beyond its confines. Particularly decisive for Motherwell's works are these intertwined internal and external perspectives, which are critical for understanding how his collages can appear to simulate a cognitive process so that neither inside elements nor the outside perimeters take priority, and thus no final conclusive position is to be obtained, as long as one participates in the inner/outer contrapuntal movement these works set up, enact, and also confound.

In addition to moving inside and outside the work of art as is the case with Motherwell's collages and paintings and their external references, his works function in a similar way to Langer's metaphors, her representational symbols, in being overall relational structures that also bespeak Whitehead's prehended energies. These culminated actual entities are eminently dynamic works of art in which the appearance of their past prehending activity remains evident in the contrapuntal ongoing interplays and tensions enunciating Motherwell's completed works of art.

Notes

1 Paul Valéry, "On 'On a Throw of the Dice'" in *Leonardo, Poe, Mallarmé*, trans. Malcolm Cowley and James R. Lawler, *The Collected Works of Paul Valéry*, ed. Jackson Mathews, vol. 8 (Princeton: Princeton University Press, 1972), p. 309.

2 Gilles Deleuze, *Difference and Repetition* (New York: Columbia University Press, 1994).

3 In retrospect, Motherwell's assent would place painting in the realm of emotions—a view to which he sometimes subscribed—and not the Whiteheadian prehended feelings he more often advocated.

4 I.A. Richards, *The Philosophy of Rhetoric* (Oxford: Oxford University Press, 1936), pp. 94 and 125.

5 George Lakoff and Mark Johnson, *Metaphors We Live By* (Chicago: University of Chicago Press, 1980).

6 Douglas R. Hofstadter, *Gödel, Escher, Bach: An Eternal Golden Braid* (New York: Basic Books, 1979).

Appendix B: Mallarmé's Materiality and Althusser's Aboutness

Mallarmé

Motherwell found that Whitehead's ideas worked in tandem with his early immersion in the French Symbolist poetry and the theories of Stéphane Mallarmé, which had taken place during a yearlong undergraduate course on this type of literature at Stanford University. Of particular significance to him was Mallarmé's revolutionary poem "A Throw of Dice" ("Un Coup De Dés") and the observation in his 1897 "Preface":

> The "blanks," in effect, assume importance and are what is immediately most striking; versification always demanded them as a surrounding silence, so that a lyric poem, or one with a few feet, generally occupies about a third of the leaf on which it is centered: I don't transgress against this order of things, I merely disperse its elements. The paper intervenes each time an image, of its own accord, ceases or withdraws, accepting the succession of others.[1]

This symbolist's reliance on the eloquent collaborative role assumed by artistic media, including the paper on which his sonnets are printed, was crucial for another of Motherwell's long-term heroes, the French painter Henri Matisse, who emphasized in his early paintings distinct breaks in the form of aerated spaces that separated the different saturated hues he was using, enabling him to state emphatically, "I don't paint things, I only paint differences between things."[2] This accent on internal rifts in works of art and the viewer's consequent need to imaginatively join them, coupled with Whitehead's view of a dematerialized universe, was so profoundly important for Motherwell that he insisted on a number of occasions throughout his life that the meaning of his abstract art was to be found in the implicit and actual relationships articulated by the distinctly different individual elements comprising it.

Insights into the expressiveness of Motherwell's collage materials, including most particularly his responsiveness to paper, are supported by his long-term interest in the poetry and thought of Stéphane Mallarmé. Motherwell's fascination with Mallarmé's poetry and this symbolist's groundbreaking ideas about the paramount role played by artistic media in the formation of modern art can be documented both in terms of Motherwell's many references to this poet as well as his collage *Mallarmé's Swan*, which he originally called *Mallarmé's Dream* (1943–1944). The difference in the two titles is significant because the earlier one connects this poet with the expatriate surrealists with whom Motherwell was becoming acquainted in the early 1940s. This first title, in fact, parallels the surrealists' own high regard for dream imagery and for the eloquent irrationality of two other late nineteenth-century French writers: in particular, Arthur Rimbaud and Isidore Lucien Ducasse, better known by his nom de plume Comte de Lautréamont. Motherwell's second title, *Mallarmé's Swan*, departs from surrealist orthodoxies and in the direction of Mallarmé's considerable role as a founder of formalist modern abstraction. The word "swan" in Motherwell's title refers to Mallarmé's famous sonnet, known as his "swan" that begins with the line "The virginal, vibrant, and beautiful dawn" ("Le Vierge, le vivace et le bel aujourd'hui") (1885). This sonnet literalizes its figurative references in terms of the poem's black type printed on white paper with generous margins. It does so by invoking two white swans. The one in lower-case indicates its earthly attachment and is buried underneath icy tundra, a figurative reference to the white paper on which the poem is presented, becoming both a metaphor and a literalization of the white support for the printed poem itself. The second one, its allegorical counterpart, is distinguished at the end of the poem by the Swan's upper-case designation and its connection with the constellation Cygnus. In French, both swans are called *cygne*, a homonym for *signe* [sign]). When spoken, this homonym *cygne/signe* refers figuratively to the sonnet's subject, its two swans, and abstractly to the poem's way of functioning as a double sign: both self-reflexively and literally by pointing to itself as a printed object as well as symbolizing its role as a sign of a transcendent experience.

If one is looking for a nineteenth-century precedence for Whitehead's views of force fields of energy (feelings) inhabiting the universe, his artistic precursor could well be Mallarmé's extraordinary sensitivity to the different times and forces that can work in concert with the poet's restricted materials of pen, words, typeface, and paper, even though Whitehead is not known to have been aware of this French poet or discussed his work. In his swan sonnet and a host of other poems such as "Sea Breeze" ("Brise Marine") (1865), referring to the daunting whiteness of the blank sheet of paper awaiting the poet's inspiration, which could transform it metaphorically into a transcendent sailing vessel or a shipwreck, Mallarmé invokes the powerfully inhibiting and also stirring force of the paper on which he writes. Even in the poet's initial stage of composing a poem, it can appear as a gaping void or an ideal space refulgent in its snowy whiteness. Sharing this highly cathected approach to paper, Motherwell recalled in 1972, "I have always been excited by the quality of various papers since childhood,...in the 1950s collage and drawing seemed sufficient to satisfy my needs for paper (as they had for years).[3]

As one might expect, Motherwell's extemporizing about the meaning of the materials comprising his art differs from Mallarmé's in terms of being specific to the intended content of his work, even though he parallels this poet's appreciation of the semiotics that can be ascribed to the artist's media before beginning to work with them. Motherwell's account of the chemical properties of the black and white paint employed in his paintings, forming a qualitative basis for understanding for his art, is a case in point. His characterization of the black and white paint he uses and the related import of these opposing values compellingly parallels Mallarmé's attitude toward paper and type, particularly when one thinks of this symbolist poet's series of poems in honor of Edgar Poe, Charles Baudelaire, and Paul Verlaine called "tombs," which mourn the death of these illustrious figures at the same time they lament the inability of poetry to do anything more than allegorize its emptiness in terms of the white void on which the poem is first inscribed and then published.

From this brief look at Motherwell's relationship to Mallarmé's poetry and their combined subscription to the basic modern aesthetic proposition of mutually reinforcing figure and form, we can conclude that his collage *Mallarmé's Swan* is not Mallarméan in terms of the specific swan referenced in its title. However, this collage can be understood as Mallarméan in a different way, providing we take into consideration this poet's associations with the color blue in a number of other poems where "*azur*" (azure) is considered metonymically related to the French word "*ceil*," meaning both heaven and sky at the same time, so one meaning cannot be referenced without alluding to the other, making this word, with its transcendent and prosaic connections, divided—a presentation of an inherent and irresolvable contradiction. The poetic resonance of *azur* and its associations with *ceil* were particularly useful for Mallarmé in setting up an ongoing contrapuntal shift between idealistic and realistic meanings, a shift he frequently employed to connote poetry's frustrated aspirations to achieve transcendent and ideal moments while being weighted down by the limitations of its self-reflexive and material form. In Mallarmé's "The Jinx ("Le Guignon") (1862), this quixotic figure herds "beggars of azure" ("mendieurs d'azur") through the world—a wonderfully poetic source for the detritus Motherwell gathers together in his collages. Noted Mallarmé scholar Henry Weinfield describes the Jinx as a personification of "a cruelly deterministic Nature that is ruled by chance and from which

God has absconded."[4] Thus, azure, with its relationship to the dual meaning of *ceil* and ongoing contrapuntal movement between elevation and mundaneness—not belonging to either realm while alluding to both—could connote modern poetry's tragic impasse.

With only a little effort, the contrapuntal or relational property of this particular blue can be seen at work in Motherwell's collage honoring Mallarmé, where it oscillates between registering a negative background space (transcendent heaven) and a positive advancing one (materialist sky). This Mallarméan orchestration of blue helps us to grasp the overall significance of this hue and its contradictory references in this and other Motherwell collages, including those works first created in the 1950s where it takes the form of actual French Gauloises cigarette packs. Motherwell's experience at the Parisian café Les Deux Magot in 1939 when he saw Picasso across the room making collages with Gauloises Bleus and whatever materials he found on the tabletop[5] can definitely be considered one of the reasons Motherwell preferred this color, and there is a certain satisfying historical correlation to this connection when being reminded that one of the few books Picasso had in his Bateau Lavoir studio in Montmartre when he created his Blue Period works was a collection of Mallarmé's poetry. Gauloises blue became one of Motherwell's favorite hues, which he used in paintings and painted collages until the end of his life as well as the favored color for the ceilings of some of his living spaces. He objectified this particular shade of blue, as he did other colors, so that it could be used in discrete segments, much like his individual collage elements, and thereby could be understood as both actual and representational as well as ideal and transcendent.

The contrapuntal movement of this azure or Gauloise blue in Motherwell's work helps us to appreciate how collages might incorporate tangible bits of evidence and shifting energies from the everyday world without being subsumed under their dominant ideologies, a problem that is particularly pertinent to Motherwell's collages of the 1950s, when he begins to incorporate and also becomes himself subject to the engrossing prehensive activity of eliciting such autobiographic bits of his own life as torn packaging with mailing labels, frequently including his address; notes written in his own hand; and the Gauloises packages that first his friend the writer B.H. Friedman smoked and later he did as well. Also, labels from the type of liquor he drank, packets of the bread he ate, and the soap he used for washing make these works highly personal. Given such revealing detritus from the artist's own life, we might well ask how these prehended references to the artist's everyday world and the ideological perspectives they assume differ when being presented in works of art; fortunately, the French Marxist Louis Althusser provides us with a carefully reasoned analysis of how ideology functions differently in art than in life.

Althusser

Althusser developed his concepts about the material effects of ideology in tandem with the ideas of his friend, the noted Parisian psychoanalyst and psychiatrist Jacques Lacan. Specifically, he relied on Lacan's theory of the mirror stage in which toddlers are co-opted by images of either themselves or others as well as by language itself, so their sense of reality depends on their imagined or intuited perception of themselves as wholes as well as members of the specific symbolic universe in which they are living. Instead of viewing the toddler as the initiator of this sequence of events, Althusser ascribes agency to the mirror and reconceives it in terms of ideologies that call forth or interpellate individuals as their concrete subjects.[6] I suggest that one can put a Whiteheadian spin on this situation by regarding interpellation—the act of being called forth as a subject—as analogous to the prehensive process. Even though Althusser's approach has proven extraordinarily useful to Marxists since it explains how subjects embrace and materialize ideologies in the course of their daily lives, it needed to be broadened in order to account for the competing ideologies that can interpellate individuals in different and often contradictory ways. The consequent necessary refinement of Althusser's basic approach to ideology, which does not reflect the real world but instead produces subjects involved in imaginary relations with others and thus is one step removed from the world, has been undertaken by Michel Pêcheux, his former student. Pêcheux has reworked the concept of interpellation so that it takes into consideration different subjectivities situated across the lines of such sociopolitical constructed identities as gender and class.[7] Both Althusser's and Pêcheux's theories about interpellation are basic to rethinking traditional views of artists and their long-acclaimed experiences as art's primary source, its form-givers par excellence. These two theorists' approaches enable us to reconceive artists as ideologically constituted subjects like everyone else and to rethink their individual autonomy in terms of the ideological discourses that are channeled through them. This reconfiguration of individual artists' roles so that they are the articulators of socially constructed views that precede them and are not their creators, enables us to appreciate the ways that Motherwell's everyday objects are not so much representative of him as they are of the already established world in which he lives—that is, the already extant realm appearing as prehended fragments in his art.

Thus far, this discussion of Althusser and the ways ideology recruits its subjects correlates with orthodox views of his theory. But I wish to diverge from this standard interpretation of Althusser and interpellation by looking at art, which a number of critics and art historians in the 1980s assumed to be a preeminently active producer of ongoing ideologies that recruited its viewers as subjects similar to the ways it functions in everyday life. Particularly notable examples of misconceiving Althusser's approach to art and ideology are found in the writing of the eminent 1980s critic Craig Owens, who contended that "to represent is to subjugate" and who writes of art's "*mobilization* of the spectator."[8] Such misconceptions as Owens's have been appealing and persuasive to many critics, historians, and theorists because they make art appear to be an eminent way to inculcate and realize specific ideologies. The consequent instrumental views of art as an ideological tool, however, have impoverished it because they obviate the crucial role assumed by *artistic form* that distances art from the machinations of particular ideologies, thereby enabling viewers to look at such ideologies as fictive and as only reflected in art rather than being concerned about being actively produced by it.

Although Althusser wrote little on art, he did summarize a number of his basic ideas about it in the brief missive known as "A Letter on Art in Reply to André Daspere" (1966), which is only rarely mentioned as a cautionary note to those who would like to view art as a means for enlisting subjects on behalf of specific ideologies. Responding to Daspere's question about whether or not art should be considered an ideology, Althusser unequivocally states that he does "not rank real art among the ideologies."[9] He then elucidates his position:

> I believe that the peculiarity of art is to "make us see" (nous donner á voir), "make us perceive," "make us feel" something which alludes to reality....What art makes us see, and therefore gives to us in the form of "*seeing*," "*perceiving*," and "*feeling*," (which is not the form of *knowing*), is the ideology from which it is born, in which it bathes, from which it detaches itself as art, and to which it *alludes*....Balzac and Solzhenitsyn give us a "view" of the ideology to which their work alludes and with which it is constantly fed, a view which presupposes a *retreat*, an *internal distantiation* from the very ideology from which their novels emerged. They make us "perceive" (but not know) in some sense from the *inside*, by an *internal distance*, the very ideology in which they are held.[10]

Since Althusser considers knowledge (as opposed to art) to be inherently structural and involved in the articulation of systems and the implicit rules "*of arrangement and combination* that gives them their meaning," he attributes this type of analysis to science, whereas art "is 'detached' from…ideology and in some way makes us 'see' it from the *outside*, makes us 'perceive' it by a distantiation inside that ideology."[11] Following this observation, I contend that the wonderfully absurd opacity of art's media and form—Mallarmé's description of paper's intervention, for example—preclude it from actually interpellating its viewers as ideological subjects because its formal means obstruct the more direct persuasiveness necessary for this type of enlistment.

In Whiteheadian terms, readers of poetry and viewers of art are prehended into art, becoming part of its separateness from the world in which it was created and part of an independently prehended formation. French philosopher Jacques Rancière, who worked with Althusser in the 1960s, comes close to ratifying this theorist's ideas about art and ideology when he views art as divided into the irreconcilable yet continually oscillating roles of its punctum (arresting form) and studium (connections with external semiotic chains of meaning that harness art to something external to itself).[12] And this oscillation, in my opinion, reinforces art's "aboutness," its distance from ideology, which it can represent as a fiction or compelling representation rather than a "reality" capable of enlisting subjects who become dedicated believers.

For our discussion of Motherwell, Mallarmé, and Whitehead, this Althusserian separation of ideology and art indicates that Motherwell's collages and paintings, like all art, provide us with enough distance so as not to be interpellated by any of the ideological traces remaining in the source material taken from the artist's daily world. We can recognize them as participants in the ideological illusions in which they have engaged, but they cannot interpellate us as they would have been able to do before being excised from the non-art world in which they formerly participated. Ideology, in this sense, becomes part of the subject but not the object of the work of art per se, since the object comprises the sum total of its prehended elements, thereby becoming a new structure or actual entity that provides the requisite distance for seeing both the subject and the ideology (or ideologies) that might have pertained to it in the world outside art. Considered in this way, art's detachment from being part of a socially ratified ideology or set of ideologies enables us to gain a much broader view of individual works of art and the world giving rise to them, as well as to ascertain, as in Althusser's symptomatic readings, how art can comprise a given problematic or discursive structures that can divulge "the undivulged even in the text it reads, and in the same movement... [relates] it to a *different text* [image/art], present as a necessary absence [of an interpellating ideology] in the first."[13] What this means for a Whiteheadian interpretation of Motherwell's collages is a clear sense that the fragments of given cultures and their contexts, which have been subsumed under a given collage's or painting's purview, can no longer be subsumed under the artist's dominant sensibility. Instead, the partially concrescing assembly of prehended energies must remain open, and the art's objectives can thus be achieved through the various self-combining forces comprising it.

Notes

1 Stéphane Mallarmé, "Preface" for ""A Throw of the Dice" ("Un Coup de Dés,") in Henry Weinfield, trans., *Stéphane Mallarmé: Collected Poems* (Berkeley, Los Angeles, and London: University of California Press, 1994), p. 121.

2 Cited in Dore Ashton, *About Rothko* (New York: Da Capo Press, 2003), p. 114

3 Robert Motherwell, "'The Book's Beginnings,' 1972" in Terenzio, ed., *The Collected Writings of Robert Motherwell*, p. 211.

4 Weinfield, "Commentary: Premiers Poëmes/First Poems" in *Stéphane Mallarmé*, p. 150.

5 Katy Rogers, "Chapter 9: Collages 1971–1991: Variation and Seriality" in Jack Flam, Katy Rogers, and Tim Clifford, *Robert Motherwell Paintings and Collages: A Catalogue Raisonné, 1941–1991*, Vol. 3, Collages and Paintings on Paper and Paperboard (New Haven and London: Yale University Press, 2012), p. 147.

6 Louis Althusser, "Ideology and Ideological State Apparatuses" in *Lenin and Philosophy and Other Essays*, trans. Ben Brewster (New York and London: Monthly Review Press, 1971).

7 An excellent example of Pêcheux's approach is found in Martin Montgomery and Stuart Allan, "Ideology, Discourse, and Cultural Studies: The Contribution of Michel Pêcheux," *Canadian Journal of Communication* 17, No. 2 (1992), http://www.cjc-onlin.ca/index.php/journal/rt/printerFriendly/661/567, consulted 9/22/08.

8 Craig Owens, "'The Indignity of Speaking for Others': An Imaginary Interview," *Art & Social Change* (Oberlin: Allen Memorial Art Museum, 1983), p. 84; Craig Owens, "The Medusa Effect, or, The Specular Ruse," *Art in America* 72, No. 1 (January, 1984): 104.

9 Louis Althusser, "A Letter on Art in Reply to André Dasperé" (1966)," http://cou rses.essex.ac.uk/LT/LT204/althusser.htm, consulted 9/15/08.

10 Althusser, "A Letter on Art in Reply to André Dasperé (1966)."

11 Althusser, "A Letter on Art in Reply to André Dasperé (1966)."

12 Jacques Rancière, *The Future of the Image*, trans. Gregory Elliott (London and New York: Verso, 2007).

13 Louis Althusser and Etienne Balibar, *Reading Capital*, trans. Ben Brewster (London: New Left Books, 1970).

Appendix C: Dore Ashton: The Arabesque

The following paper was presented at the symposium "Homage to Dore Ashton," held at The Cooper Union, New York City in December, 2015.[1] It focuses on the still-too-little appreciated poetic device known as the arabesque. I am including it as an appendix because it provides a way to demonstrate how some visual art is able to utilize Whitehead's prehensive energies and Mallarmé's ongoing dialectics between his poetry's materialist printed form and its transcendent aspirations. An understanding of the arabesque is also helpful in diagramming Motherwell's collage aesthetic and its oscillation between his media and his qualitative insights.

According to the *Oxford English Dictionary*, the word "arabesque" originally referred to Arabs or the Arabic language. Subsequently, "arabesque" signified decorative patterns of interlacing foliate shapes, remarkable for their ornateness and complexity. This term also describes an elaborate figure of speech, comprised of intricate arrangements of words and concepts, indicative of thought's movement from one form to another, constituting a verbal wit capable of breaking through frames and condensing differences. Both the visual design and the verbal word play making up these two definitions of arabesque involve viewers and readers in the concentrated process of teasing out the intricacies of simulated movements, a process endowing this involved form with a dynamic and also a feeling of unending fecundity or perpetual becoming. Although the arabesque has a long lineage—Viennese art historian Alois Riegl conjectured it may have been the first decorative pattern humans originated—its modern theoretical antecedents are nineteenth-century romanticism and symbolism, particularly the literary theories of Samuel Taylor Coleridge, Edgar Allan Poe, Charles Baudelaire, and Stéphane Mallarmé that Dore Ashton has repeatedly acknowledged as important for her criticism. Among Ashton's many references to the arabesque is the following where she writes,

Delacroix taught Baudelaire to seek the musicality of paintings, urging him to back away from the painting until the subject receded and only the overall arabesque was visible. The notion of the arabesque itself, common to both arts, took on almost mystical overtones later in the century, as the Symbolists sought to wrest from the pictorial mode its innerness and its rhythmic power.[2]

For Ashton and the nineteenth-century individuals she cites, the arabesque describes a movement from a work of art's titular subject to its formal means, and it sets up an ongoing contrapuntal movement between the two, so that the work of art is able to communicate its theme, even as it comments on its mode of construction. The situation is akin to Laurence Sterne's editorializing in *Tristram Shandy*, where readers are made privy to the novel's narrative strategies, even as these tactics are being enacted.

The arabesque's oscillation between a given work's theme and its formal means are succinctly summarized in Ashton's observation, "These paintings [by Philip Guston] are thought but they are also paintings."[3] This stress on Guston's finished works as both idea and paint is indicative of Ashton overall hermeneutic approach that differs markedly from that of her older fellow critic Clement Greenberg. For Ashton, a modern painting is certainly an empirical object in the world, but since it is involved in thought, it is never completely present, as Greenberg believes. Moreover, unlike Greenberg, whose formalist criteria assumes the weight of overarching and unwavering laws for judging all modern art, Ashton believes the critic's "clearest approach can be only through contemplation of the individual art's work."[4] Her criticism is remarkable for its "searching discussion,"[5] and she employs the essay form as an investigative means for entering the never-ending process of understanding both the work of art and her relationship to it, a connection she characterizes in terms of being "an *activity* of my culture, a culture that I not only inherited but also shaped." Also hermeneutic is Ashton description of ideal critics as "respond[ing] to the arts with the sum of their personal culture...[and] seek[ing], not a method, but an entry into the universe of the particular work of art."[6] As she has counseled, a critic "must never become entangled in a system. It is a kind of damnation."[7] Anti-idealist to the core, Ashton is engaged in the process of coming ever closer to the "circumference of the magic circle around the artist which keeps us always at a distance from the inviolable point"[8] yet always involved in the process of trying to come closer to it.

While Ashton employs the concept of an "inviolable point" in order to emphasize the artist's sacred personal space, many of her essays extend this concept to individual works of art and poetry and their visual and verbal silences, which she views positively as perpetually mysterious. Ashton respects silence as forming the in-between space comprising an arabesque, the mysterious synapse between words, colors, forms, shapes, and thoughts that serve as both external and internal breaks, providing opportunities for the affective bridges viewers are able to collaborate in forming. In her important work on Mallarmé, Ashton writes, "The white of the page, to which he [Mallarmé] was always so sensitive, would provide the rests, pauses, silences that his ideal of musicality in poetry required."[9] In other words, Mallarmé's poetry forms a richly embellished interlace around the subject of nothingness, sometimes wittily connecting the figurative caesura of the white pages on which his sonnets were published—that is, the perpetual mystery forming the soul of his poetry—with "the canvas of a sail [,] with the white of a painter's canvas"[10] or white sea foam.

For Matisse, who illuminated some of Mallarmé's poems, the white paper on which he worked serves as an arabesque, an arresting break between form and content, an insight Ashton readily acknowledges when citing Matisse's statement:

> I obtained my goal by modifying my arabesque in such a way that the attention of the spectator would be interested as much by the white pages as by his expectation of reading the text.[11]

According to Ashton, Matisse's emphasis on such rifts, which he subsumes under the heading of "arabesque," are a means for encouraging viewers' felt response to art "through establishing proper relationships."[12] Ashton is careful to note that Matisse's insight, "I don't paint things. I only paint differences between things,"[13] has a source in Mallarmé's emphasis on relationships," a perception supporting her deduction: "Matisse's esthetic was based on the principle that feelings could be summarized, symbolized through establishing proper relationships."[14] Such relationships have also been crucial for Motherwell's collage aesthetic that is informed by Matisse's example as well as by Mallarmé's poetry and Whitehead's theories.

In conclusion, Dore Ashton has enriched our understanding of the work of certain modern artists through exploratory essays predicated on a number of tensions that she seeks to understand rather than reconcile. For Ashton, the arabesque's overall contrapuntal shift between form and content serves as an ongoing and open-ended dialectic that endows individual works with a sense of movement and vitality. The contradictions Ashton projects and manages to keep suspended provide arabesque-like openings that enable readers to participate in the dynamic moves she so admirably frames, thereby encouraging them to take responsibility for their own hermeneutical perspectives.

Notes

1 My thanks to Michael Corris, who was a key organizer of this excellent symposium, which Ashton was fortunately able to attend.

2 Dore Ashton, "Criticism and Arts" in Dore Ashton, *The New York School: A Cultural Reckoning* (Berkeley and Los Angeles, Oxford: University of California Press, 1972), p. 316.
3 Dore Ashton, "A Response to Philip Guston's New Paintings" in Ashton, *The New York School: A Cultural Reckoning*), p. 18.
4 Dore Ashton, *The Unknown Shore: A View of Contemporary Art* (Boston and Toronto: Little, Brown and Company, An Atlantic Monthly Press Book, 1962), p. vii.
5 Ashton, *The Unknown Shore: A View of Contemporary Art*, p. vii.
6 Ashton, "Criticism and Arts" in Ashton, *The New York School: A Cultural Reckoning*, p. 315.
7 Ashton, *The Unknown Shore: A View of Contemporary Art*, p. vii.
8 Ashton, *The Unknown Shore: A View of Contemporary Art*, p. x.
9 Dore Ashton, "Mallarmé, Friend of Artists" in Dore Ashton, *The New York School: A Cultural Reckoning* (Berkeley and Los Angeles, Oxford: University of California Press, 1972), p. 263.
10 Ashton, "Mallarmé, Friend of Artists" in Ashton, *The New York School: A Cultural Reckoning*, p. 276.
11 Dore Ashton, "The Other Symbolist Inheritance in Painting" in Dore Ashton, *The New York School: A Cultural Reckoning* (Berkeley and Los Angeles, Oxford: University of California Press, 1972), p. 287.
12 Ashton, "Mallarmé, Friend of Artists" in Ashton, *The New York School: A Cultural Reckoning*, p. 267.
13 Ashton, "Mallarmé, Friend of Artists" in Ashton, *The New York School: A Cultural Reckoning*, p. 268.
14 Ashton, "Mallarmé, Friend of Artists" in Ashton, *The New York School: A Cultural Reckoning*, pp. 267–268.

Index

For Product Safety Concerns and Information please contact our EU
representative GPSR@taylorandfrancis.com
Taylor & Francis Verlag GmbH, Kaufingerstraße 24, 80331 München, Germany